Becoming An Angel of Soul Justice

"With Listening Heart, Listening Ears, Listening Eyes"

Dora B. Durante

Angel of Soul Justice
"Listening Heart, Listening Ears, Listening Eyes"

Copyright © 2022 by Dora B. Durante
All rights reserved by Dora B. Durante

Permission
This book is printed and bound in the USA.
All rights reserved. Dora B. Durante

Printed in the USA

All rights reserved

Washington DC Maryland USA International

Dedication

I dedicate this book to my beautiful and loving mother, Maeola Brown, who prayed without ceasing and had journeyed with me through this process of becoming who it is God had assigned me to be. Even after your death, I could feel and hear your soothing and comforting voice accompanying me on my drive home. Every seed planted, since you gave birth, every prayer prayed on my behalf, know that I love you with all my heart, mind, soul and spirit. You were my greatest supporter and inspiration. I miss you every day, but rest with peace knowing that you are at peace, resting in the Master's bosom.

Acknowledgments

To **My Lord and Savior, Jesus Christ,** thank you for never giving up on me. For holding onto my hands even when I wanted to let go of your hand. Thank you for trusting me to share your wisdom, comfort and strength to your precious creation, knowing that I too am an imperfect image of humanity.

My Husband, Henry White, thank you for taking up the mantle of reading and editing my written assignments and for encouraging me to continue the journey that God had placed me on, even when I wanted to give up.

Rosalia Elizabeth Durante (Mama D), thank you for always having a word of wisdom on your lips to share every day until you breathed your last breath on August 9, 2020 at age 103.

Alonzo McLeod, thank you for being my friend and tennis buddy for three years; being the person who listened to all my cares, concerns, desires and wishes. Thank you asking for my hands in marriage and being my devoted partner for one year, three months and 16 days, showing me what earthly unconditional love truly looked like; for reading and providing feedback to written assignments; for holding on to my hands and never letting them go until you breathed your last breath, April 28, 2007, still loving and encouraging me, even as you knew you were being summoned to your final resting place.

Latrice Brogsdale Davis, thank you for being a prayer partner at work and for your continuous pushing and encouraging me to write my story; the story of a faith-filled journey to follow the Will of God.

My Wesley Ladies – Rev. Renee Jones, Michelle Ellington, and Alison Lewis, thank you for just being you. Thank you for making a way to meet for brunch, lunch or dinner, when there was a need for feeling connected; for covering me following the loss of my beloved Alonzo, and encouraging me to finish my journey and have an expectation that I would indeed one day be what it was that God was calling me to be. I love you dearly, like my own blood sisters.

Rev. Dr. Benjamin Foust, even though you are no longer with us physically, your presence is felt in spirit. Thank you for being my spiritual mentor encouraging me to take the necessary steps to move forward on multiple fronts. Your words of wisdom continue to remain with me. Thank you for being the first one to send a reference response for the start of my graduate school journey on the road to becoming a licensed counselor.

Rev. Dr. Lee P. Washington, thank you for everything, especially the opportunity to witness the spirit of humbleness in greatness. You provided letters of reference to both graduate programs and during the loss of Alonzo, your quiet outreach to others provided sources of strength, guidance and directions to help me move forward. Your way of in the words of my mother, "speaking the unadulterated truths" without holding back as given to you from our Heavenly Father. Thank you, thank you, thank you!

Chieblo Quantae Durante, my son, thank you for one day reminding me that God uses us wherever He places us, even in a federal job environment; and that there are many there who need someone to just listen. And in His own timing, He will let us know when it is time to depart.

Tami E. Johnson at The Brand Studio of the Greater Washington Metropolitan Area, thank you for being more than just a photographer, for capturing life's unique moments as artwork in an authentic, professional and loving manner that allows it to be a resource that can be used for multiple arenas.

Ramon and Janie McGee, thank you for being led by the Holy Spirit to inspire me to stop hesitating and to move forward to share with the world my story of how God never fails us even when we fail to follow through on our promises to do His will.

Table of Contents

Becoming An Angel

Of Soul Justice

Preface

My metaphor is *"Angel of Soul Justice"*. What is Soul Justice? What is justice? What is soul? When I think about soul justice, I think about the repairing of the inside of someone who is suffering due to loss; loss of identity, dignity, humanity, freedom, and a number of other perceived and real losses. When I refer to "soul", I reference it as the principle of life, feeling, thought, and action in humans. God "breathed the breath of life" into Adam and he became a "living soul" (Gen. 2:7) (Achtenemeier, Boraas, Fishbane, Perkins, & Walker, Jr., 1996). Definitions of justice that are closest to my concept include equitableness, or moral rightness and just dealing or treatment: to seek justice. According to Plato, *"Justice is Harmony" (Book IV, 434 b.)*, (Aquileana, 2014) "Justice is an order and duty of the parts of the soul; it is to the soul as health is to the body."

I define soul justice as *the true and lawful healing of one's brokenness from the inside out; a healing process from pain and destruction that produces life* (joy, peace, happiness, and self-worth). Soul Justice is finding a true sense of worth that will enable one to redirect or channel negative energy into positive energy; to let go of self-pity and low self-esteem; to understand that one is justified in their search to recognize their significance in a world where equality or equity continues to appear out of reach. Soul Justice is the regaining of a voice that was previously silenced through continuous physical, verbal, and/or emotional abuse. It allows one to move beyond the past and present and realize hope in the future. Soul Justice is the armoring or empowering of individuals so they can become fully visible in society. Soul Justice allows one to perceive his or her pain and engage in a process to encourage one to move beyond the pain he/she experienced and declare freedom from being stuck in pain.

As Dr. Martin Luther King (1963) stated in his, "Letter from a Birmingham Jail"; "Injustice anywhere is a threat to justice everywhere" (p. 1). Injustice begets the loss of freedom (imprisonment or enslavement of the mind, body, soul, speech, or other actions or reactions). Wherever and whenever freedom is denied, the entire society is endangered. This is evident across this nation and the world today with the many instances of suicide bombings, African American males unjustly killed at the hands of law enforcement officers; Black on Black crimes, co-workers inflicting harm in the workplace, and numerous other acts of injustice. Loss is plentiful and healing appears limited.

CHAPTER 1

Introduction

As I look back on all of my career choices, family, society, religious, relationships, and life experiences, I realize that these have all contributed greatly to my formation process of becoming a pastoral counselor. These include chemical lab technician, chemical research analyst, high school science teacher, tennis coach, census worker and manager, and student; relationships with family, including in-laws, society, marriages, deaths, and other events beginning with my childhood.

Historical Events

I was born in 1952 in Marion, South Carolina and raised in the Cherry community of Charlotte, North Carolina from the age of two by a single parent (mother) with two sisters. Two brothers, my oldest and youngest siblings were raised in different households. I was raised Pentecostal Holiness. While in undergraduate school, I started attending an African Methodist Episcopal church and maintained membership within that Christian religious affiliation until 2021.

Childhood

As a child, I spent the summer in Marion, South Carolina with my grandmother from the moment I became able to labor in the grasslands. I was joined by my two sisters and youngest brother and cousins. I worked in numerous fields to include cotton, tobacco, soybeans, etc. According to the standards of society in terms of socio-economics, we were poor. I did not know that we were poor since we had more food than we could eat; lots of laughter, and all of the necessities of life. However, this was a period of obvious inequality, when Blacks, regardless of their age were called boy or girl by the dominant society and segregation was evident on all fronts (water fountains, bathrooms, restaurants, public transportation, shopping opportunities, etc.).

During the sixties, I lived through a number of high-profile assassinations; John F. Kennedy on Friday, November 22, 1963, Dr. Martin Luther King on Thursday, April 4, 1968, and Robert F. Kennedy on Thursday, June 5, 1968. These assassinations caused much confusion, discouragement, hurt, anger, and pain. Every time there appeared to be progress in advancing opportunities for all of society, someone at the forefront of this struggle would be violently killed. The world was seeing the actions of individuals who were suffering from unresolved issues, those seeking their own soul justice, and trying to deny others their soul justice. And there I was, not sure of my place or role in life.

I recall my joy and proudness as a sixth-grade student in 1963, when my teacher taught us to recite and dramatize James Weldon Johnson's (1927, renewed 1955), *The Creation,* especially the last two standards that read:

"Then God sat down; On the side of a hill where He could think, By a deep, wide river He sat down; With His head in His hands, God thought and thought, till He thought, I'll make me a man! Up from the bed of the river God scooped the clay, and by the bank of the river He kneeled Him down; and there the great God Almighty, who lit the sun and fixed it in the sky, who flung the stars to the most far corners of the night, who rounded the earth in the middle of His hand; this Great God, like a mammy bending over her baby, kneeled down in the dust toiling over a lump of clay till He shaped it in His own image, Then into it He blew the breath of life, and man became a living soul. Amen."
(Johnson, 1927, renewed 1955, pp. 20-21)

God created man (me) to be a living soul and now mankind was doing everything possible to remove the breath from God's image to make it a dead or nonexistent soul. I, along with millions of other school children were pledging our allegiance to the United States Flag every school morning saying: "I pledge allegiance to the flag of the United States of America, and to the republic for which it stands, one nation under God, indivisible, with liberty and justice for all." It was a difficult time trying to understand if there was something wrong about wanting to be equal, a part of this one nation. Why did so many individuals have to lose their lives, if we were indeed all created in only one image, God's image and were seeking to serve this God equally in this *yet to be* United States of America? Was I not good enough or undeserving of happiness only because of the color of my skin? What had I done wrong?

Following elementary school (sixth grade), I attended the all black Second Ward High School (grades 7 – 12). The summer before my ninth-grade year, there was a court order to separate high schools into junior high (grades 7-9) and senior high (grades 10-12). I must now attend the majority White, Piedmont Junior High. This would be my first opportunity to gain more insight as to why my people, including myself were regarded as inferior to the dominant society, unworthy of sharing public facilities, educational opportunities and many other inequities. For an entire summer, I suffered uneasiness (feelings of insecurity, unworthiness, doubt, and rejection) about this new journey that I, along with my friends, was about to encounter. There were thoughts of moving from the top ten percent of the class to the bottom ten percent of the class. On the first day of school, we made the long two mile walk to Piedmont Junior High School; no buses were assigned to take us to the school. Fear and tension increased with each step. My first class, following homeroom was science, one of my favorite subjects. The teacher, a White man, began to ask questions to review our knowledge base. He asked the first question twice. I knew the answer, but since I saw no other hands go up, there was doubt. After he asked the question a third time, I raised my hand. He pointed at me for the response, and I wanted to die for bringing attention to myself. I finally found my voice and shared my answer and he said, "That's right, you are right." I almost passed out. After answering a few more questions, I slowly began to regain confidence and a sense of self-worth. I felt life and not death. My thoughts then turned inward trying to understand why the news media and others created barriers that inflicted self-doubt, a sense of unworthiness, hurt, pain, and other negative internal feelings that had generated such a crippling fear. I returned to Second Ward High School the next year as a sophomore with renewed energy and self-worth.

As I was preparing to enter my senior year of high school, there was a court order that called for forced busing to integrate schools, thus, the closing of the *beloved* Second Ward High School. I attended the previously all White Harding High School, but this time, my fears were not so crippling. Even in the midst of mild doubt about math and science classes such as physics and trigonometry, I felt certain that I could compete and was worthy, regardless of others' attitudes, expectations or non-expectations of success or failure. I did not allow challenges, name calling, and a part-time job, to prevent me from graduating with honors. Both of the above experiences were critical to my understanding of loss and the return of dignity, humanity, and self-worth; and critical to my desire to help others navigate through those troubling waters, an Angel of *Soul Justice* for all, regardless of race, ethnicity, or other identities.

The slogan of the Civil Rights movement "We Shall Overcome" for me was more than a song just for the movement. It represented a symbol of hope and future fulfilling of the scripture and promise that God loved all that He created. This represented an affirmation that God had not created His African American children to be subjected as sub-humans for an eternity to feel as though they could not even look to the future for redemption in the eschatology. It represented the promise and hope of soul justice for everyone, regardless of race, creed, color, or gender.

A Visitation

Before leaving Charlotte to attend college at North Carolina Central University, I had my first intimate encounter with the "Audible" Lord. I was a teenager in the back yard of my mother's home hanging clothes on the clothesline when I heard this voice saying; "Go Preach My

Gospel". I had just been saved and had received the anointing of the Holy Spirit. I looked everywhere to see if one of my friends or anyone else was trying to play some trick on me. Again, I was the only human being in the vicinity. It was very frightening, until I recognized that it was the Lord speaking to me. So, I said, "Lord, I will spread your word, but it will be as a missionary. I will be the best missionary possible." And then I was off to college. Thus began my spoken commitment. However, my participation in civil rights activities (nonviolence training, marches, get out the vote, and sit-ins), college, and other not so productive life activities during my college days, seemed to overshadow this spoken commitment to God. As I look back, I realize that through those activities, God was continuously training me to be an advocate of soul justice, fighting to help heal broken systems (separate and unequal facilities, including education), broken men, women and children to include perpetrators and victims. Once I graduated from college, I realized that I was not as close to the Lord as I had been prior to going to Durham, NC. Actually, I had such a good time in college that Church was not at the top of my list of priorities. This was revealed to me during a period of fasting and prayer during a revival. I quickly recommitted my life to Christ and joined the missionary society hoping to make good on my promise. I settled into this role, teaching Bible study, serving as director of the youth program that was an extension of the missionary society and singing in the choir, feeling all the time that I was fulfilling what was required of me by the Lord.

Community

It was normal for my grandmother, mother, and my generation to face and manage adversity with the confidence of overcoming as a family or communal affair. The communal response of African American teachers, neighbors, friends, ministers, and others represented the essence of the African proverb *"Because we are, I am. I am because we are"* (Shopshire & Stroghlin, 2008, p. 126). When individual members of the family or community underwent adversity, all were affected and would spring into action while joining in prayer for relief and guidance. This sense of pastoral communal care embodied Ubuntu – connectedness, a web of interrelatedness (Shopshire & Stroghlin, 2008, p. 127). Prayers were accompanied with active participation of physical, financial, and emotional support from family, the local church and community; true and active missionary work, not just spoken commitment. The gifts and resources of the community were used to address hurts and struggles of individuals and to engage systems and structures that caused the harm. This spirit of communal care shaped my understanding of how to confront crises.

Education and Early Employment

I received a Bachelor of Science in Chemistry from North Carolina Central University with minors in Biology and Mathematics in 1975. I worked ten years in the chemical industry and after learning of a serious sensitivity to organic chemicals following a period of illness, transitioned to the educational field as a high school teacher where I realized my greatest strengths, leading and motivating others. Witnessing the excitement in students' eyes and bodies as they grasped concepts of biology, chemistry, physics, and physical science that they previously had feared, reminded me of how I had tackled my crippling fears as a student. As a teacher (a helping professional), I devoted my time to helping high school students recognize their potential and encouraged them to tackle challenges outside their comfort zone and not allow others, including teachers, high school counselors, and friends to keep them from reaching for the stars, just as my teachers, parents, church and community members had challenged me. This meant calling upon internal counseling friends that included attending, observing, following, responding, and influencing to be an effective change agent for my students, parents, and others, including my son who was a high school student.

Relationally, I experienced four marriages. Ironically, my first husband was an African Methodist Episcopal minister who died suddenly in 1983 from a massive heart attack at the age of 39. As the wife of a minister, I was called upon to lead the missionary society and young people's department with a mission to continue the ministry of Christ by service and witness to the world: *"to travel far and wide, wherever helping hands and willing hearts are needed, spreading the Good News to persons of all stations, races, and places. The good deeds of this ministry are widespread and plentiful. From visiting the ailing in hospitals and the infirm in nursing homes, helping the homeless, and organizing blood drives and emergency services, to raising money for scholarships, aiding the victims of famine and war through overseas missions, and hosting Christmas gift-giving programs for needy children, preparing the youth and young adults through age 26 for the Christian leadership roles of tomorrow —the members are here, there, and everywhere, honoring Christ and the local church"* (Women's Missionary Society, 2014). At the age of 30, I became a single parent of a nine-year-old, African American male child.

To supplement my income as a single parent, I expanded my hobby of sewing into a part-time self-employed business, worked part-time with the United States Census Bureau during the 2000 Census while continuing with my full-time employment as a chemical lab technician, teacher, coach, and junior class advisor. I also served as a tennis instructor, line judge and chair umpire for the United States Tennis Association for Junior Championships and hosted USTA Junior Championship tournaments, with all that money used to support a grass roots Junior Tennis Academy. Following the 2000 Census, part-time/ full-time worker for the Census Bureau, happenstance occurred. I was encouraged to apply for a permanent job with the United States Census Bureau, which I did. I was offered and accepted the job with the Census Bureau as a Supervisory Survey Statistician at the Charlotte Regional Office where I provided oversight to approximately 352 staff that included both office and field workers. Witnessing low morale in the office, I led a program that encouraged staff on all levels to equip themselves with skills to place them in positions for promotions as they pursued opportunities to improve their personal and work environments.

My key roles and responsibilities as a Supervisory Survey Statistician were to train, guide, support, and continually encourage workers in an environment where rejection and hostility were commonplace. I used my skills to communicate, encourage, and place myself in environments that were uncomfortable in order to meet work goals.

My second marriage December 1996, ended in divorce due to insecurity. January 13, 2006, at the age of 54, I married my best friend of three years, Alonzo McLeod. There was complete union of the body, mind and spirit; never an argument. He died suddenly in my arms on the tennis court in 2007. I married my current husband, Henry "Hank" White August 2010, following the 2010 decennial census.

Witnessing the Work of God

During the 1990 Census, I served as a part-time enumerator, and Crew Leader. I recall a Friday evening before the scheduled closeout of the 1990 Census non-response operation; I received a phone call from one of my enumerators who reported that he had the flu and could not complete his assignment of approximately 100 cases. These were located in an identified hard-to-enumerate community. I was the closest census worker to this location. I prayed an extra prayer that morning before I drove approximately thirty miles to this huge apartment complex. Once I was at the location, a woman opened the first door. I immediately showed my identification and apologized for interrupting her Saturday morning. She knew my intent because she had previously been visited by a census worker. I explained the importance of participating in the census and how funds would be appropriately allocated to improve not just her life but those of her children and grandchildren and others in the community. She finally agreed to complete the questionnaire and then stated that she would call her neighbors and tell them to cooperate by completing their interviews. I thanked her, and before I could knock on the next door, it opened and that person completed the interview. Individuals, who had not previously responded to the census, began to come out of their homes and stand at their doors waiting to complete an interview. God had sent me to the door of an angel who would help make my assignment an easy assignment. I completed the enumeration for the entire complex (96 interviews). God was continuously affirming His purpose and His promise to be with me at all times when I am walking according to His purpose.

The final case on the enumeration assignment was the home of a gentleman that was down the street from the complex. A note stated that the head of the household had threatened to shoot the next Census worker who knocked on his door. After driving to the location, I sat in my car for a moment, looked around, and prayed that I would not have to enter this home. After noticing what appeared to be signs of a family with children, I could not leave. I knocked. A gentleman answered the door, looked at me, and said "I'm sure that you know what I told the other people that came to my door." I said "Yes, I received a note, but I am hopeful that you will change your mind." I started explaining how important it was that I made sure that his daughter, who was peering around the corner, received the same opportunities to enjoy community and educational activities as other children. He finally asked me to stop talking and just tell him what I needed. He completed the interview. I went back to my car and cried, thanking God for sending *words* and His angel to protect and cover me. This man along with the citizens of the apartment complex who may have experienced some type of loss just needed to hear and know that somebody cared beyond a paycheck; that someone cared about their humanity and dignity regardless of an assumed apathy.

Closer to Answering the Call

Leading up to the 2000 U.S. Decennial Census, I was stuck in the middle of deciding whether to continue to pursue teaching, or to pursue starting a business using my sewing skills, specifically, my formal wear designer knowledge. January 1999, a friend was looking for part-time employment. I reminded that friend of postings that the Census Bureau was looking for part-time workers. The friend presented a laundry list of reasons for not taking the test, including anxieties about not being able to pass the test. I encouraged them to put aside that list and promised to accompany them to the test location. I then went into the location with them and was handed a test, which I took to encourage the friend to take the next step. I took the test without any intent to become involved with the census as I had already laid out plans for my next venture in life, starting my own sewing business. Several days later, I received a phone call from the local census office informing me I passed the test and asking if I was ready to start working. I declined, explaining the reason I took the test. I received a second call. This individual told me they noticed I had previous census experience and would like for me to reconsider helping them with several address list update programs. This time I gave an affirmative response as the friend I had encouraged to take the test had called to share they too had received a call but they were not going to take the assignment unless I agreed to do the same. My mind was thinking all sorts of thoughts, including repeating my negative response, but I felt an obligation to help my friend take that critical step forward and not miss that window of opportunity to accept this part-time employment. I accepted the offer and began part-time work off and on with the Census Bureau for various programs. This allowed me to still continue designing formal wear and other sewing projects as part-time employment until the summer of 2000, when I accepted a full-time temporary employment opportunity as a Regional Technician traveling to and from Area Census Offices with the Charlotte Regional Census area until September, 2000. In November 2000, as stated above, I applied for, was offered and accepted the job with the Census Bureau as a Supervisory Survey Statistician at the Charlotte Regional

Office. In 2002, I transferred to the Washington Metropolitan Area, U. S. Census Bureau Headquarters in Suitland, Maryland, where I have worked for the past 20 years, as of October 10, 2002. In addition to managing a staff of nine, I have served as a mentor for both the Census Bureau and the Department of Commerce Mentoring Program, mentoring individuals across all seven Bureaus and advocating for individuals continuously seeking soul/futuristic justice. Moving to Washington, DC metropolitan removed me from a busy environment where I constantly allowed myself to be pulled in multiple directions to prevent hearing the voice of God.

A Second and Third Visitation

In 1985, living in Greensboro, NC, the Lord again visited me and repeated His command to, "Go Preach My Gospel." Having been a minister's wife, I was really not trying to go into the ministry as a pastor. This time my reply was, Lord, if you really want me to Go Preach your Word, you must come down here on earth and make your request to me in person. On September 12, 2004, my 52nd birthday, the Lord again visited me saying "Preach My Gospel". It was a Sunday morning and I was in church being attentive to a spiritual message that was being delivered by our pastor, Reverend Dr. Lee P. Washington, and this interruption from God was very distracting. I was able to finally block out that message from God, but only for a short period that day. While on my way driving home, God returned with persistence, and I was annoyed with His persistence, stating, "So, I see you're back Lord." When I arrived at home, I was surprised to learn that my car door would not open. This was a first. I did everything I could to open that door, especially since it was one of those hot September days. Finally, I relaxed and said, "God, I apologize for my disobedience, but if You will let me out of this car, I will not delay Your will for me. Immediately, my car door opened. God had the final word that day. I went inside to my apartment, turned on my computer and started looking for a school/ seminary to attend to start my journey of Studying His Word to show myself approved.

On Friday, September 17, 2004, God sent another confirmation through one of the speakers for the Reid Temple AME community-wide revival. I was sitting in the church and asking God to please send me some form of confirmation so that I would know that I was making no mistake. He sent not one, but two signs as confirmation. First, the glass window behind the Choir loft appeared to light up symbolizing a cross. I asked the person sitting beside me if they saw it. As I began to touch them, I heard God say, this was only for you. The person sitting beside me had no idea what I was talking about. I initially felt foolish. But then I was comforted because I realized it was God giving me another confirmation of His love for me. You see, one of the things that had been holding me back was thinking I was unworthy to be a spokesperson for Him. I cried. Second, the revival speaker, Rev. Jamaal Bryant, the revival speaker came forth with the second confirmation that night. Following a prayer, the reading of the scripture and giving his topic, he stopped. He stated that God had asked him to deliver a message to someone who was searching for a confirmation from Him to enter into His ministry. He said, "The Lord wants me to tell whoever the person is that "Yes" I am asking you to go into the ministry and you need to not sit in doubt." Wow! Amazing ways to receive confirmation! I cried a little then, hearing God say, "It's time for you to forgive yourself. I forgave you a long time ago, even before you asked for forgiveness." Following the service, I ran out of church that rainy Friday night with tears streaming down my face, and went forward diligently seeking for the right seminary to fulfill His command. I needed no additional confirmations. The Holy Spirit through Rev. Washington guided me to apply to Wesley Theological Seminary. So, at age 52, I stopped thinking that I was not worthy to serve as someone to be a voice for God.

After graduating from Wesley with honors while still working full-time, I assumed that it was time to take a rest. God and I were not on the same page. He kept me sleepless in Maryland. During my second class at WTU, God confirmed my ministry was not in a pulpit within the four walls of a brick church building. He said, "My people are hurting from the inside out. Your ministry is to help my people heal." Following many sleepless nights, I engaged in conversations with my Pastor Washington and my husband who both encouraged me to go back to school, stating that this was God's design; Pastoral Counseling was in my deoxyribonucleic acid (DNA). Also, I nor my mind was not getting younger.

Significant Losses

As stated above, I personally experienced several significant losses: loss of identity, dignity, humanity, confidence, and acceptance, and loss of loved ones that include two husbands, mother, father, spiritual director, and a son who lost self-confidence. The experiences and skillsets developed or enhanced from those losses contributed greatly to my formation process and understanding of loss as I sought to become a Pastoral Counselor to help others heal from their losses.

As stated earlier, my first husband was an African Methodist Episcopal Minister who died suddenly in 1983 as a result of a massive heart attack at the age of 39. At that time, we were separated. In March 1997, I received a message that my father had died from a massive heart attack. The Sunday morning prior to my father's death, he called me and shared so much regarding his joys, concerns, and other desires, including things he wanted members of his family to have when he died. He kept me on the phone so long that I missed church that day. This was a strange exchange of information because my father was not sick. I informed him that he should document his desires in a Will. That week after returning home from a tennis match as coach with my girls' team and attending a PTA meeting, I learned my father had died through several phone messages. My family allowed me to uphold his wishes in the absence of a Will. In 2000, my second marriage ended in divorce mainly because of insecurity and inequality (unequally yoked). God did not allow me to mourn that loss. I did not view the divorce as a loss but as a blessing. January 13, 2006, at the age of 54, I married my best friend of three years, Alonzo. Alonzo supported and challenged me to stay the course with my theological studies. There was complete union of the body, mind and spirit; never an argument. April 28, 2007, only one year, three months and sixteen days, he died in my arms on the tennis court without experiencing any previous sickness. On the morning of the one-year anniversary of Alonzo's death, the Holy Spirit communicated a message I realized that only God could enable me to comply, "Keep placing one foot in front of the other and continue to actively use the gifts that I have placed in you to reach out to help others in their search for soul justice: dignity, humanity, acceptance, self-worth, self-identity.   If you are obedient, I, through the Holy Spirit will supply you with the strength, energy, peace, and wisdom to complete each of my tasks." Knowing that God's word does not come back void, I remained focused through excruciating pain. I learned that even, in the midst of pain, the Holy Spirit allows us to experience soul justice (joy, fellowship, peace, accomplishment, comfort, self-worthiness, etc.). One day I spoke to my Senior Pastor about the pain I experienced from losing two husbands with such suddenness. I asked him why God was allowing me to suffer so much loss. Why had God given me an individual who loved me unconditionally and then snatched him out of my life? He told me that I should seek counseling. I refused to comply. I now wonder what approach a counselor would have taken to help me journey through my pain. What could I have gained to pass on to others? Whereas, I had a great source of support, including my spirituality, I know that many who experience loss have no support.

My spiritual director, Reverend Dr. Benjamin Foust, who died in 2009, encouraged me to heed my calling to attend WTS and he made himself available whenever I called. He was an active listener, listening to God with one ear and listening to verbal and nonverbal communication. He encouraged and challenged me to love God with all my heart, soul, and mind and to continue to lean and trust Him regardless of what happened in life (death, sickness, loss of job, etc.). Because of that relationship, I gained the benefits described by Calhoun that included: "walking with a companion who can help me hold my soul before God, notice my experiences with God, recognize God's voice in my life, and find Jesus in the wounds as well as the joys." His death left a void in my heart, but I could always hear his voice telling me to keep moving forward toward my God appointed destiny.

On my fourth wedding anniversary (July 28, 2014), my mother transitioned to her heavenly home. She had an unwavering faith in God. My husband, Hank, and I had traveled to Charlotte, North Carolina to be with her as she prepared to move into an independent living facility. As she and I sat alone the third day of her residing at this facility, she shared details with me about her love for each of her children. She encouraged me to press forward and told me how glad she was that my husband had traveled with me this time. I had traveled alone each time I visited earlier that year. She then informed me that she was going to take a nap. That nap turned into an eternal sleep. My mother served as a buffer to eliminate stress and misunderstanding as I worked to unload a few overwhelming responsibilities, mainly with my son. She had an open, warm, and positive channel of communication with her children and grandchildren. Mom would call me around 9:15 PM or 9:45 PM to accompany me on the way home from night class while at WTS and Loyola University. During a period of stressful communication, my son stated, "Mom, I can't talk to you right now, but I can talk to Grandma. I can talk to Grandma because she listens without giving opinions or being judgmental." I am not sure this was what I wanted to hear, but it provided a sense of comfort knowing that during our period of rough bumps, there was someone in the family that he felt he could reach out to. I was not aware my statements were judgmental. However, it was my son's perception that mattered at that time. When I spoke to my mother concerning my son's comments, she stated, "Honey, there are times I have to just sit and listen without providing any comments when speaking to each of you. I sense when each of you would not be receptive to any advice. I wait for the opportunity to present itself for me to speak on the subject; a time when you are more receptive to words of wisdom." "Wow," I said to myself. I pray that one day I too will be just as in tune with when to speak and when to just listen, especially with my son. My mother-in-law (Mama D), who celebrated her 104th birthday prior to her death on August 9, 2020, constantly reminded me of resilience to press forward in the midst of death, and other struggles.

Journeying Through Seminarian Studies

My journey through Wesley Theological Seminary (WTS) to complete the required 60 credit hours to receive a Master of Science Degree of Theological Studies started January 2005, taking only one class to get my brain acclimated to studying at that level. My journey included the following courses: Spring 2005: Introduction to New Testament: Epistles; Fall 2005: Introduction to New Testament: Gospels, Church in History: Early Reformation; Spring 2006: Introduction to Hebrew Bible II, Church in History: Reformation to the Present; Summer 2006: Philosophy for Theology; Fall 2006: Introduction to Hebrew Bible I, Systematic Theology I; Spring 2007: Christian Education & the Black Experience, Systematic Theology II; Summer 2007: Life and Writings of Martin Luther King, Jr.; Fall 2007: Counseling Skills for Pastoral Ministry; Spring 2008: Spiritual Disciplines, Leadership & Administration for Small Churches, Christian Ethics & World Religion; Summer 2008: Acts & Pauline Epistles, Sociology of Religion, Songs of Zion: Spirituals; Fall 2008: Pastoral Care & Identity, The Lively Word; Spring 2009: Pastoral Care, Marriage and Families, and Urban Ministry Action.

During my enrollment at WTS, I took advantage of the opportunities afforded by the Washington Theological Consortium to attend other theological schools of diverse faith traditions in support of Christian ecumenical unity and interfaith understanding. I completed two Pastoral Care classes at Washington Theological Union (WTU), a Roman Catholic graduate school of theology and ministry, in Washington, DC, that increased my awareness of the importance of interpersonal and professional boundaries in the ethical practice of pastoral care and counseling and personal psycho-spiritual well-being for counselors and clients in the practice of pastoral counseling. Introduced me to counseling skills that I applied to manage families and couples in conflict, and provided opportunities to explore and develop an applicable understanding of the dynamic of family resilience.

My study of the New Testament Gospels and the Old Testament enlightened me to the criticality of analyzing a text with thoroughness prior to utilizing it to deliver an intended message of hope and salvation. It taught me to take the time to read, read, read, and reread a text for understanding.   In addition, the historical context allows one to vicariously, place self in the situation of the original intended audience and opens one's eyes as to what circumstances one may use a text to help shape the fabric of societies positively wherever and whenever called upon.

The Counseling Skills for Pastoral Ministry course was following the death of Alonzo. The goal of the course was to develop the attitudes, knowledge and skills necessary to be effective and affective pastoral counselors. The objective of the course was that at the end of the course, students would be able to demonstrate: A basic level of competence in the skills of active listening, client-centered empathy, unconditional regard and in-depth communications in pastoral settings; their knowledge of and appropriate, skilled responses to some of the most common types of pastoral needs and crises that arise in ministry; An increased awareness of the importance of interpersonal and professional boundaries in the ethical practice of pastoral care and counseling; An ability to maintain personal psycho-spiritual well-being for themselves and their clients in the practice of pastoral counseling.

When my husband suddenly died on April 28, 2007, I was in total shock and filled with pain, but knew I had to press forward. God said, "Dora, do not sit in a corner feeling sorry and grieving your loss, but reach out and help others. If you are obedient, I will provide you with the strength and courage to press on and that reaching out to help others will be the source of your healing." This class served as an additional source of that inspiration and strength. I quickly recognized this class was God's orchestration and therefore, looked forward to being in attendance and gaining all the knowledge available to fulfill God's request and to do it effectively. The reading assignments provided insight into the skills necessary to become an effective counselor in the theological arena and served as a source of my own healing. I went in search each day for the tools to help me reach out to others as commanded by God and to continue my spiritual growth, knowing that if I did not complete my process of healing, I would be unable to help others move from where they are to where they want to grow. My experience would become a resource to build upon. I found myself beginning to do more active listening instead of listening with anticipation of getting my opportunity to speak and therefore miss some of the details of what others had stated.

My Spiritual Disciplines course informed me of the need to develop my own "Rule of Life for Spiritual Transformation" a rhythmic awareness of God's work in and through me to accomplish his purpose. My desire was to "live a sane and holy rhythm that reflects a deep love for God and respect for how he has made me," (Calhoun A. A., 2005) e.g., establish a 'rule of life.'

Several of these disciplines I selected to help me meet my desire for life-giving connection with God and authentic spiritual transformation included: celebration, confession and self-examination (self-awareness and self-management), prayer (contemplative, meditative, vocal, etc.), discernment, fasting, journaling, Sabbath, silence, solitude, witness, worship, and spiritual direction. Consistent practice of these disciplines helped me achieve my desire to "live a sane and holy rhythm that reflects a deep love for God and respect for how he has made me," (Calhoun A. A., 2005) e.g., establish a 'rule of life.'

I started practicing the twin disciplines, silence and solitude as a jump start to promote spiritual growth in my pursuit of godliness. Silence and solitude combined with attention to the presence of God are the starting point for all other practices. They place us where we may listen to hear God's perspective on our world, our circumstances, our goals, and our relationships. This was my beginning.

Practicing the Sabbath helped fulfill my desire to set apart one day for simple rest and quiet worship of God.

As a leader in both the organized religion and other cultures, it was important to practice and have an appropriate view of self, combined with the capacity to help others. To manage feelings, I needed to be aware of my emotions (depression, anger, hostility, grief and loss, fear, and bitterness) and understand their origin, self-awareness. According to McNeal, one's success grows out of their ability to have a "well managed life." (McNeal, Practicing Greatness: 7 Disciplines of Extraordinary Spiritual Leaders, 2006) I needed to have a "well managed life."

The discipline of journaling helped me to be alert to my life through writing and reflecting on God's presence and activity in, around, and through me. Wolpert points out that the practice of journaling bridges two worlds, "the world of God's Word and the world of our words-in an attempt to communicate to ourselves and others that which God would have us hear and know. I long to take on the rhythm of intentionally journaling to enable me to capture the Words I hear from God that I know He provides for me to share to others.

Keeping the practice of worship as a part of my rhythm fulfills my desire to honor and adore the Trinity as the Supreme treasure of life with intentional consistency. To worship God means to ascribe the proper worth to God, to magnify (or to make big and enlarge) His worthiness of all praise and adoration. Worship is: focusing on and responding to God; done in spirit and truth; expected both publicly and privately; and a discipline to be cultivated (Calhoun A. A., 2005).

Even though one of my strongest desires is to practice Sabbath, as a Christian, I still long to practice the discipline of service by being a witness, revealing the life-changing love of Jesus to others (Whitney, 1991). Every Christian: is expected to serve; is gifted to serve; is mandated to serve; should serve out of gratitude; and every Christian should serve out of love. Motivation to serve should be obedience to God, gratitude, gladness, forgiveness, humility and love (Calhoun A. A., 2005). As leaders and Angels of Soul Justice, we have a responsibility to encourage others to become empowered by fulfilling their God given purposes reminding them that we are all gifted and expected to serve God.

Onward to Pastoral Counseling

As stated above, God did not allow me to rest after I completed my degree at WTS. The interests generated while taking the pastoral care classes at WTU were still burning. God had shown me that He needed me to help individuals heal from a holistic perspective, not just a theological perspective. God presented experiences that helped me understand that even though I was "assumed" educationally, equipped to *rightly divide* His word, my journey to completing His Will was unfinished; helping individuals suffering complete their healing. He wanted and needed me to be equipped with knowledge of interpersonal and professional boundaries in the ethical practice of pastoral counseling, personal psycho-spiritual well-being for myself and my clients, and the skills to manage individuals, families and couples in conflict.

My next step meant applying to Loyola University's Pastoral Counseling: M.S. – Ph.D. Combined Program. I submitted the below essay with my application on October 24, 2011.

I, Dora Brown Durante, am a member of Reid Temple African Methodist Episcopal Church where my faith identity is aligned with the Apostles' Creed. I am an active participant of several in-reach and outreach ministries. These include the Reid Temple Mass and Chorale Choirs, Class Leader, Master's Touch and Mentoring Program for College students.

Since 1975, I have embarked upon three successful careers: the chemical industry, education, and the federal government. In spite of my successes, the questions that keep arising are, "am I fulfilling my dreams or God's assignment; are my accomplishments the results of a Spiritual Gift or developed talents?" While it is important to have a successful career, it is most important to understand that we all have an earthly ministry to fulfill; to exemplify the ministry of Christ. His earthly ministry was expressed through an ethical ministry of words as expressed in the beatitudes, parables, etc., a healing ministry of touch and being touched (his healing), a militant ministry of expelling evil forces (exorcism of demoniacs, whipping the moneychangers), his ministry of prayer, etc. My decision to study Chemistry in college was based on achievements in science and mathematics classes throughout elementary and secondary school. Failure in any subject was not an option for me or my siblings. Allergic reactions from many of the organic chemicals forced me away from industrial chemicals in 1987 into the educational field as a teacher on the secondary level where I discovered my greatest strengths, teaching and mentoring. Recognizing the excitement in students' eyes and bodies as they grasped concepts of biology, chemistry, and physical science that they previously had feared to tackle was a delight.

To supplement my income, I worked part time with the Census Bureau during the 1980, 1990 and 2000 censuses during my employment in the two above careers. During the later stages of the 2000 Census, I made a decision to consider a career with the Census Bureau, thus my present employment.

Even though I left the structured teaching and mentoring environment I continue to participate in activities that enable me to help others recognize their full potential. These include: church youth director, tennis coach, math and science tutor, mentor for the Department of Commerce, the Bureau of the Census, and college students, and Class Leader ministry. Mentoring is multi-directional; it helps me grow both personally and professionally.

In 2004, God in His own way (I will share the story if asked) firmly instructed me to enroll in a post-secondary institution to "study His word to show myself approved". I enrolled at Wesley Theological Seminary in the Master of Theological Studies degree program. When God assigns us a task, it requires preparation. We are not born qualified, so we must become qualified, which is why God takes us through seasons of preparation.

God tells us to get in a boat and row to the other side, knowing that we will experience storms in the midst of our passage. Storms include spot quizzes. God snatches things from us to see how we handle them. On April 28, 2007, my husband of one year, three months and 16 days suddenly died in my arms on the tennis court. God, the Almighty Father carried me through that storm, kept me on course, and protected my mind, even as I continued to work full time. I graduated from Wesley with honors on May 11, 2009.

On September 13, 2011, I received yet another spot quiz. My new husband underwent a minor surgical procedure. While receiving post-operative instructions, his spirit suddenly departed his earthly body. We had been married one year, one month and sixteen days. I turned to God to remind Him of a bargain and promise. The bargain was, "God, I will go through this doctoral program, if you promise to keep this husband, my best friend here to walk with me and to celebrate with me the completion of this assignment. True to His promise, God brought my husband back; God's word does not return void, Isaiah 55:11 (Coogan, 2001). I thank God for sending me another partner to support me and to provide confirmation of God's love and greatness and of the journey before me.

My studies at Wesley afforded me a basic level of competence in pastoral counseling to be a more effective and affective class leader/pastoral counselor, mentor and witness in the Master's Touch ministry. The following classes: Counseling Skills for Pastoral Ministry, Pastoral Care of Marriage and Families, and Pastoral Care and Identity enhanced my skills that include active listening, client-center empathy, unconditional regard and in-depth communications in pastoral settings, increased awareness of the importance of interpersonal and professional boundaries in the ethical practice of pastoral care and counseling, the ability to maintain personal psycho-spiritual well-being for myself and my clients in the practice of pastoral counseling, counseling skills to manage families and couples in conflict and the opportunity to explore and develop an applicable understanding of the dynamic of family resilience.

My responsibilities of pastoral care as a lay worker at Reid Temple AME church for the last two years have required me to assist individuals from a Holistic perspective, providing physical, mental, and spiritual encouragement to individuals and families going through. Whereas, my studies at Wesley enhanced my ability to process and integrate information, I was not equipped with a level of clinical knowledge that would allow me to fully integrate theology and the social sciences skillfully to provide adequate mental encouragement in a pastoral counseling setting.

My journey through Loyola will expand my knowledge base of the principles of pastoral counseling while I explore wider dimensions of the counseling relationship through opportunities that will exhibit appropriate techniques within said relationships from a psychological and Christian perspective, a Holistic perspective.

Even though I am committed to one faith community, as Disciples of Christ we must be servant leaders operating within our divine assignment to the Universal Church. In Jonathan Kozol "Ordinary Resurrections" we see the universality of the church in the lives of economically disadvantaged young children witnessing to someone that is not a professed Christian. Where these kids lacked in economics and social activities, they made up for in their connection with God, communicating through the Holy Spirit. Their message strongly encourages me to stay prepared to be obedient to the great commission to assure the Gospel of Jesus Christ is practiced in my every day actions in any work environment and to be prepared to attend to the whole body, regardless of race, ethnicity, social, economic, or political status. It is Christ's intent for us to practice a ministry of justice and love for all humanity and non-humanity.

I concluded my studies at Wesley with a thesis entitled, "The Interrelatedness of Theology, Sociology, and Ecology: An exploration of the role religion plays in the interaction and action of humanity and the natural world". Jurgen Moltmann and Guthrie Johnson assert that the whole of creation is valued by God; and if humanity has an affinity with all creation, humanity too would value all God value. This I affirm.

Finally, my goal is to intentionally focus on actively listening to God to align with my divine earthly assignment and not my developed talents. This includes receiving whatever tools, training resources, and encouragement are required to operate within my divine assignment to perform Kingdom tasks from a Holistic approach. I expect that my studies at Loyola will generate an interest in me to create or explore new knowledge in the study of spirituality, religiosity and mental health.

Prior to my enrollment in Loyola's Pastoral Counseling Program, I reflected on my accomplishments, recognitions, and awards, specifically the two Bronze Medal Awards I received for leadership during the 2010 Census. Instead of feelings of satisfaction, I had some feelings of discomfort. My deepest desires (greatest sense of meaning and contribution) had been to simply help others in their search for futuristic and soul justice, not to fill a wall with certificates and awards. Thus, I began the contemplation and search for divine confirmation. Did my theological studies satisfy the plans of the *Master Designer?*

In response to my question regarding my purpose for continuing studies of Pastoral Counseling, I reflected on the wisdom of Ellen G. White (2011), co-founder of the Seventh Day Adventist Church,

"For what purpose are you seeking an education? Is it not that you may relieve the suffering of humanity...You know not to what position you may be called in the future. God may use you as He used Daniel, to take the knowledge of the truth to the mighty of the earth. It rests with you to say whether you will have skill and knowledge to do this work...He can help you to adapt yourself to the line of study you take up. Make it your first interest to gather up right, noble, uplifting principles. God desires you to witness for Him. He does not want you to stand still; He wants you to run in the way of His commandments."
(White E. G., 2011, p. 485)

Journeying as a Pastoral Counseling Student

I started classes in the Loyola University Pastoral Counseling: Master of Science Degree Program, January 2012, to be obedient and run in the way of God's commandments. God's commandment at this time was that I equip myself with Pastoral Counseling skills regardless of intuitive skillsets. Maybe, He required me to be a deliberate thinker with an enlarged knowledge base.

As part of my Pastoral Counseling internship, I encountered victims and offenders, both male and female, four days a week, each seeking their own soul justice. I often reflected on my survival through unjust experiences, a survival of loss experienced over a lifetime. I then reminded myself that I survived those losses because opportunities and individuals equipped me with the strength, courage, and resilience to overcome and regain peace to exist as a productive force in society; the same kind of peace these victims and offenders are seeking. Many of the individuals I saw as an intern had no strong positive internal locus of control or external support.

I am assured without doubt that my productivity exists only because God continues to keep me in perfect peace. My favorite scripture, Philippians 4:6-7, (NIV) reads, "Do not be anxious about anything, but in every situation, by prayer and petition, with thanksgiving, present your requests to God. And the peace of God, which transcends all understanding, will guard your hearts and your minds in Christ Jesus" (Coogan, 2001). Each time doubt or fear enters my mind, I immediately hear God saying, "I've got you; keep moving forward, and I will give you the *words* to say. I will always be with you, but you must always remain with me." I wish this soul justice for others, especially victims and offenders of domestic violence. This does not mean things will be easy at all times, but it also does not mean that one is not deserving of inner peace and, knowing that things will get better. I am grateful that God has instilled in me an inner peace to be able to sit and listen to individuals as they share painful and frustrating experiences in search of soul justice. His peace enables me to distinguish His voice and allows me to rightly divide the word of God, experiences and knowledge from Pastoral Counseling training and theological studies at the right time. As I stand in the gap, I also know that God requires self-care of me so that I can be replenished and ready at all times to stand in the gap for others.

So, what time is it for Dora Durante? Now is the time to become a Pastoral Counselor, an Angel, God's messenger of Soul Justice.

"Now is the time...to discover people's back stories. Learn to discover people's backgrounds. Ask and listen for the clues. Their histories reveal many things. They can explain fears and prejudices. They can unravel mysteries. They can give you warnings; or insights." (Lindsay, 2009, p. 170)

SPIRITUALITY OF PASTORAL COUNSELING

CHAPTER 2

As I entered into my studies at Wesley Theological Seminary and the Pastoral Counseling program at Loyola University, I was keenly aware that my journey through both of these iconic institutions would be alongside individuals with differing faith or other spiritual beliefs. One's faith foundation is a critical lens factor in how one receives and perceives others and their activities. However, this does not mean that one cannot have flexibility to allow room for understanding other faith foundations or spirituality.

My faith foundation, which is a result of many trials and tribulations, is Christianity. Personal revelation and theological explorations that include scriptures and various theological readings allow me to affirm all twelve articles of the Apostles' Creed.

I Believe in God the Father Almighty, Maker of heaven and earth. And in Jesus Christ His only Son our Lord; Who was conceived by the Holy Spirit, born of the Virgin Mary; Suffered under

Pontius Pilate, was crucified, dead, and buried, he descended into Hell, the third day He rose again from the dead, He ascended into heaven, and sitteth on the right hand of God the Father Almighty; from thence He shall come to judge the quick and the dead. I believe in the Holy Spirit, the Universal Church; the Communion of saints; the Forgiveness of sins, the Resurrection of the body, and the Life Everlasting. (Historic Church Documents, 2006)

The above twelve articles of the Apostles' Creed have served as a source of soul justice: a source of h*ealing of brokenness from the inside out, a tool of life* (joy, peace, happiness, self-worth), an understanding of my justification in my search of significance in a world where equality or equity appeared to be out of reach, and the armoring or empowerment to become and remain fully visible in society and to move beyond pain. This is the foundation for which I approach pastoral counseling. As shared in Maynard & Snodgrass (2015), in regards to one's view of God, individuals and counselors could view God as judge, God as love, God as parent (mother and father), God as benevolent (but senile) grandfather, and God as oversoul (pp. 63-65).

I have personally proclaimed the words of the Apostles' Creed as my belief for twenty-nine years even though I have recited the words for thirty-six years. When I first started uttering these words as part of my worship experience in 1971, I was a student at North Carolina Central University in Durham, North Carolina. At Saint Joseph African Methodist Episcopal Church these words were initially a matter of routine recitation because I was experiencing a faltering of Christian faith as a result of a painful experience while a member of the Apostolic Holiness Faith. It is very hard to affirm a faith when one is wrestling with problems of injustices, especially from an environment one assumes to be trustworthy. However, my experiences through past and then current social, economic, and political situations kept reminding me of the evidence of the love and power of God as attested in the Bible, the inspired word of God. The utterance of the words of the Apostles' Creed, "was crucified, dead, and buried..." would pierce my heart even as I tried to think of these as mere words of expression. In 1978, following a two-week period of fasting and seeking guidance, I again experienced the reassuring presence and anointing of the Holy Spirit, a presence that helped me to feel secure, justified and prepared to again handle the injustices of society as a youth leader of the church. From that moment, the Apostles' Creed has served as a personal testimony of my Christian beliefs just as it has for many others including our forefathers, since it was adopted a half century or so from the last writing of the New Testament. Throughout my theological and pastoral counseling studies, I have continued to expand my understanding of the Apostles' Creed through class readings, discussions with fellow classmates and instructors, closer examination of the Word, ongoing personal experiences, and how it helps me relate to the suffering of many. It is this understanding that allows me to sit before my clients with empathy, nonjudgment and unconditional positive regard when they enter my presence seeking soul justice from their perspective of the pain and suffering, they are experiencing.

God as Parent (Father and Nurturer)

Starting with article 1 of the Apostles Creed, *"I believe in God the Father Almighty, Maker of heaven and earth,"* this article expresses my belief in the existence of a true and living triune God; a God that is almighty and powerful as evidenced in the splendor and beauty of his creation all around me, not just humanity. As I call Him Father Almighty, I affirm that he is the *Creator* of all things, that is in heaven and on earth. The whole of creation is valued by God; and if humanity has an affinity with all of creation, humanity too would value all God values. Therefore, as an Angel of Soul Justice, I too must demonstrate that same measure of love for all of creation.

When I say "Father," I use it in terms of God as mother, father, brother, sister, comforter, etc. As a mother, He is a nurturer. As a Father, He is a passionate protector and Judge. As a brother or sister, He is a friend I can relate to. And as a comforter, He is my all and all.

When I think of God as a parent, I am reminded of working with Client A who grew up in a strict Catholic home. She reported to counseling because of her awareness of a strong underlying anger toward her husband caused by his inactions to help provide for the family for approximately five years. Even so, she had continued to defend him in front of family and friends, when financial concerns or questions about his health would arise. Client A grew up in a household where the actions and communication informed her that she should not kick a man when he appeared to be down. She also wanted to be able to 'honor her man" according to her faith belief. She had resisted coming to counseling, postponing several times before she actually kept the appointment. Client A reported that in spite of everything that was going on in her life that caused anxiety or other unhealthy pressures, she understood that God was the source of her strength and had continued to bring her through tough times. Her key concern now was disappointing God, her Father by leaning on external devices, and counseling, to help her with her problem. This appeared to align with research on African American females and their faith identity.

> "Black women have been the most mistreated and scandalized in U.S. society and culture as they wrestle both individually and collectively with the triple jeopardy of racism, sexism, and classism...it is no wonder that black women...would seek out their faith to find relief, reprieve, resolution and redemption. An absolute trust in a higher power has been a truism for centuries for African American women. They feel that their God is one they know intimately; guides, cares for, and chastises those He loves. They talk to God and He talks back" (DeBose, 2012).

To help this client in her search for soul justice, I employed bibliotherapy that was grounded in a faith foundation identical to this client to help her realize that "when we quit those things that are damaging to our souls or the souls of others, we are freed up to choose other ways of being and relating that are rooted in love and lead to life" (Scazzero, 2010). This is what any parent (mother and father), especially, our Heavenly Father would want for his/her child. It was my belief that God had sent client A to me to help me understand my role as an Angel of Soul Justice and to help her to see that God has angels here on earth who are here to serve as His intercessors to help His children who experience hurt and pain.

Stating Article II, *"I believe in Jesus Christ His only begotten Son our Lord"* affirms my belief that Jesus Christ is the Son of the true and living God. "For God so loved the world that he gave his only begotten Son, that whosoever believeth in him should not perish, but should have everlasting life" (John 3:16, NIV). The not perishing extended not only to the eschatological but also to the present. Soul Justice in the form of Love for all of humanity was demonstrated by God the Father. As a believer, I too have to practice that same form of love; unconditional positive regard for all of humanity.

"I believe Jesus Christ was conceived by the Holy Spirit and born of the Virgin Mary." With this statement (Article III), I affirm my belief in the incarnation, the becoming flesh of the divine Logos in Jesus Christ, the begotten Son, establishing the union of the divine and human natures in one person. Born of the Virgin Mary, speaks to God's understanding and confirmation of the nurturing needs of humanity.

God as Love

"I believe Jesus Christ suffered under Pontius Pilate, was crucified, dead, and buried and descended into Hell." As stated above, this Article IV, expressing the suffering of an innocent Christ under Pontius Pilate that led to His death keeps me humbled in moments when I feel I am being misjudged, misunderstood, and inflicted with injustices. The sufferings of Christ are the suffering of one who was blameless, but because of His love for humanity would pour out His life 'His glory' to come to earth to

become a sacrificial atonement, to restore the broken relationship between God and humanity, broken because of my sins and transgressions. For this, I am exceedingly thankful.

As an Angel of Soul Justice, I have a responsibility to help mankind to restore broken relationships with families and individuals. The suffering of an innocent Christ should only serve as a metaphor of redemption (soul justice), not communicate a message that suffering of any kind is to be glorified. I agree with the statement that, "if Christianity is to be liberating for the oppressed, it must be liberated from a theology that glorifies suffering" (Carlson & Rohn, 1989). All of humanity should be viewed as equal, no slaves, and no macro or micro populations where macro stands for the dominant society in terms of wealth and power. My earthy ministry, as an Angel of Soul Justice, is to exemplify the earthly ministry of Christ. Christ's earthy ministry was expressed through the following ministries: an ethical ministry of words as expressed in the beatitudes, parables, etc., a healing ministry of touch and being touched (his healing), a militant ministry of expelling evil forces (exorcism of demoniacs, whipping the moneychangers), his ministry or prayer, etc. (Williams, 1993). It was Christ's intent for us to practice a ministry of healing, helping others to understand the source of their pain, and restoring justice and love for all humanity and non-humanity.

When I speak of his descending into Hell, it demonstrates my agreement with Paul when he said, "Therefore it is said, when He ascended on high, He made captivity itself captive; He gave gifts to His people," When it says, "He ascended," what does it mean but that He also descended into the lower parts of the earth" (Ephesians 4: 8-9, NIV)? It is also said that when he descended into Hell, He broke chains and set the captives free. "The Spirit of the Lord is on me, because he has anointed me to proclaim good news to the poor. He has sent me to proclaim freedom for the prisoners and recovery of sight for the blind, to set the oppressed free..." (Luke 4:18, NIV). In the counseling world, the oppressed is any client that enters a counselor's door. The Pastoral Counselor, the Angel of Soul Justice, then engages in a process that provides hope, mirroring the indestructible twin towers of "grace and mercy".

A Promise Kept

"I believe on the third day Jesus Christ rose again from the dead." This expression, Article V, affirms my belief in Christ's promise and scripture forecasts of His resurrection. It provides me with the strength and courage to stand boldly in the face of injustice and affirm my steadfast hope and faith in the true and living King. Basically, it provides the hope that a day will come when all of humanity will be free of pain and suffering. This is a process of soul justice, one perceiving his or her pain and engaging in a process that encourages one to move beyond the pain he/she experienced and declare freedom from being dead or stuck in pain.

This article gleams light on an eschatological hope that many of our clients may cling to when they are in the midst of grief for a lost loved one. This hope may serve as a source of comfort that life may not cease with death; that there is justice in the resurrection and they will see their loved one in the eschatological future. As a Pastoral Counselor, my hope is that the therapeutic process will allow my clients to find soul justice in the present and future while they are on this side of eternity.

In Article VI, I express my belief that *"Jesus Christ ascended into heaven, and sitteth on the right hand of God the Father Almighty."* For me, the scriptures bearing witness first to the resurrection of the crucified Lord, then to the ascension of Jesus Christ into heaven completes the resurrection and restores the broken relationship of the Son and the Father. Christ regaining His rightful seat at the right hand of God the Father, the place of highest glory, power and satisfaction expresses the honor and dignity of the Person of Jesus Christ where none other qualified and provides me with a sweet, sweet assurance of justice.

God as Judge

"I believe Jesus Christ shall come to judge the quick and the dead." Article VII expresses the eschatology or as Moltmann phrases it, it points to the future and reminds me that one day Christ shall return to judge my actions along with those of all my enemies and community of believers. The one thing I must remember, I am commanded to preach the gospel to the people and to testify that Jesus Christ is the one ordained by God as judge of the living and the dead. Preaching the gospel is done on whatever platform God provides as His pulpit. Everyone who believes in Him receives forgiveness of sins through his name, (Acts 10:42-43, NIV). I am thankful for God's immanence whereas he liberates me from having the responsibility to judge my adversaries. I would probably not be so gracious. Therefore, I am thankful He placed this in the hands of His Son, the one and only worthy Judge. This helps me to be available to all of humanity regardless of race, age, gender, sexual orientation, ethnicity, or any other cultural distinctions. God said that everything He created was good and that He has purpose for everything

He created. *"In Him also we have obtained an inheritance, being predestined according to the purpose of Him who works all things according to the counsel of His will"* (Ephesians 1:11 NKJV). Because God has purpose for everything He created, it allows me to be an authentic Angel of Soul Justice, knowing God is Judge.

When I think about God as Judge, I am reminded of Client B, who was court ordered to attend an abuser intervention program. Even though he was court ordered to attend the program because of abuse, he shared that he was experiencing anxieties associated with knowing that his son was placed in a foster home because of the actions of both his mother and his father. Client B was trying to gain custody of his son and had to undergo unannounced drug tests. His anxieties were tied to his desire to not fail his son, stating this was critical because he grew up in a household away from both his mother and father. Our counseling strategies included Client B learning how to manage his anger and better understand the underlying symptoms and causes of domestic abuse. Client B reported abusive behaviors that involved yelling, name calling, and physical abuse that included knocking out his son's mother; inflicting pain and suffering on others. When Client B reported that Jesus Christ was his role model, this provided an opportunity to focus on the actions of Jesus Christ versus his actions. While acknowledging that Christ exemplified moments of anger; Jesus turning over tables in the Temple, Client B was able to share that Jesus' anger did not cause physical harm to others and that Jesus always communicated the purpose of his anger in a controlled manner; effective communication. Jesus Christ as Judge practiced controlled anger and judged all of His children; all of humanity, with love.

"I believe in the Holy Spirit." Article VIII affirms the presence of the Holy Spirit that I experienced on that Friday night in Charlotte, North Carolina prior to attending college that has been instrumental in continuously transforming me even to this day. As I worship God, I strive to allow the Holy Spirit free will in all my actions and pray that it is evidenced by others through the works of the Spirit, which is displayed, hopefully, as the Love of God burning in my heart like fire; my show of humility; true kindness to all people; true love that involves a freedom that allows all around me to think of God or a higher power; and the illumination of the mind that leads me and others to an elevated state of ecstasy; joy, peace and happiness. My experiences in interacting with the Holy Spirit reflect Moltmann's (2014) definition of the Holy Spirit; "The Holy Spirit is the loving, self-communicating, out-fanning, and out-pouring presence of the eternal divine life of the triune God, a God who sees no differences when He looks on our pain and suffering and dispenses with healing" (p. 188).

God as Oversoul

Instead of *"I believe in the Catholic Church",* Article IX of the African Methodist Episcopal Church was changed to *"I believe in the universal church."* The term universal church provides no denotation of any specific denomination of believers. All believers who declare him to be 'our Lord' are included in this expression. The universality of the church means the church is made up of all people, and not reserved for a certain class of people, race of people, and national origin of people. It speaks to the church being present in all parts of the world. God as oversoul is an expanded "understanding of the indwelling of God to all living things"

(Maynard & Snodgrass, 2015, p. 65). In Kool's "Ordinary Resurrections" (2001), we see the universality of the church in the lives of economically disadvantaged young children witnessing to someone that is not a professed Christian. Where these kids lacked in economics and social activities, they made up for in their connection with God, communicating through the Holy Spirit. They allowed me to witness the language of hope and reality in the midst of the disadvantage; to get a glimpse of soul justice. The church is alive wherever the examples of Christ are represented. The children were the disciples letting their light shine even in the midst of darkness. Their message strongly encourages me to stay prepared to be obedient to the great commission to assure the Gospel of Jesus Christ is practiced in my every day actions to every creature to provide the assurance that they too are entitled to the saving grace of our Lord and Savior Jesus Christ, regardless of social, economic, or political status. As the church of Jesus Christ, we must make the effort to look out for those who are without, suffering; oppressors, perpetrators or victims.

When I speak of the universal church, I speak of being available to serve the masses, whomever and wherever they may be; multiculturalism and diversity, locally, regionally, nationally, or internationally. While participating in a developmental assignment in the Office of Africa with the Department of Commerce International Trade Administration agency in 2007, I was afforded the opportunity to share with United States and African officials, concerns about ways to improve the welfare of all citizens on the African continent, not just Ambassadors and Ministers, and other elect. My pastoral counseling understanding and life's experiences as a child, young adult and even now, keep me aware of the need to continue to seek ways to stay aware and push to impose policies to help make a difference (advocate). I was afforded that opportunity again in 2010 when the U.S. Census Bureau selected me to go to Rio de Janeiro, Brazil in May 2010 to help their government plan for counting individuals experiencing homelessness in their upcoming Census. My assignment was to share knowledge of ways that government could design a program to help count this population; with the understanding that all humanity mattered, and to suggest ways to make sure this was completed in a sensitive manner; a manner in which this population would not experience injustice from a political and required process.

Pastoral Counseling training means equipping one to be in a state of readiness to attend to the needs of the universal church regardless of race, class, ethnicity, sex, gender, or sexuality. To better equip myself and to be obedient to the Great Commandment, in October 2014, I traveled to Malawi as part of a mission trip in partnership with the Somebody Cares (SC) Malawi team whose mission statement reads:

> *"To proclaim and establish the profound dignity of every human being because our human dignity comes from God our creator not man! Nothing we go through or experience (deprivation or suffering) can remove this dignity – for we are always precious in the sight of God. Somebody Cares brings hope to the dying, sick, suffering and most of all the ones most affected -vulnerable and orphaned children and widows. SC seeks to restore a society that is broken and a generation that is dying. SC provides education and creates awareness on HIV & AIDS*

in order to impact society at the core (the family) and get involved with caring and building of communities so they are empowered." (Somebody Cares Malawi, 2014; Amundson, Harris-Bowlsbey, & Niles, 2014)

Wow! Whereas the entire mission statement is powerful, the first two sentences that speak to dignity are most powerful to me. In Malawi, we visited and prayed with adults with AIDs, women groups working with their individual growth activities (IGA), helped to decorate a village community center for the opening ceremony, and interacted with women and girls in their agricultural IGA; all of which were what we term "well below the poverty scale." However, I was so caught up in the industriousness of these men, women, and children working continuously with dignity regardless of their assigned or self-imposed task and their level of socioeconomic status. This dignity; human dignity must be acknowledged when any of our clients (perpetrators or victims) who all may be suffering from their soul justice come and sit across from me seeking their own sense of justice. Otherwise, change or soul justice will remain out of reach; unachievable.

"I believe in the Communion of Saint; the forgiveness of God." The first part of Article X, *the Communion of Saint,* expresses that the community of believers, those who strive to live godly in Jesus Christ, and to be holy as He has called us to be, ought to fellowship in harmony one with another, with no respect to denominations, sex, gender, ethnicity, or societies. All members in communion with the Father, the Son, and the Holy Spirit, whether scattered across various countries, are all of one mind and are knitted together by a common faith and mutual sympathy just like the members of the living God. The communion between God and

humanity represents the mutuality that should exist throughout humanity and the rest of creation, which could serve as an instrument of peace throughout creation. There would no longer be oppressors and those being oppressed. There would be true freedom and true justice in terms of equality and equity just as the triune God desires for his creation. Instead of inequity or biases, there would be equity in determining who would gain entrance to that seat across the table from a fully equipped Pastoral Counselor, a considered Angel of Soul Justice. All of God's creation qualifies.

God as Benevolent (Senile) Grandparent

"I believe in the Forgiveness of sins." This second part of Article X has taught me that sincere forgiveness leads to salvation. The forgiveness I received was not because of anything I have done but because of the love and free gift purchased by the blood of Jesus Christ, "the Lamb of God that taketh away the sin of the world" (Romans 5:19, NIV). When I think of forgiveness, I am always reminded of Sojourner Truth's last interview with her former master (slaveholder) who confessed that 'slavery was the wickedest thing in the world, the greatest curse...' What a confession for a slave to hear from a slave master. With that confession, his sins were forgiven. It is hard to imagine slaveholders, those who kept others from voting, who treated others as inferior (lynching, separation of public facilities), who kept others thinking they were inferior, and those who carried out genocidal campaigns deserving an opportunity for forgiveness, even though I believe Christ came to forgive the sins of all, not just my sins.

My faith has helped me to adjust this frame of thinking. Just as I have been given the opportunity to ask for forgiveness of my many sins, oppressors of injustice also have that same opportunity to change their lives, pray, and ask God for forgiveness regardless of the gravity of the sin. When speaking of the wicked, I have to remember that salvation allows us to live in the present and not in the past. Christ loves us all despite our faults. He allows grace to flow freely to us. According to II Corinthians 5:17; (NIV) "If anyone is in Christ, he is a new creation; the old has gone, the new has come."

When I state Article XI, *"I believe in the Resurrection of the body"*, I affirm my belief that one day there will be a resurrection of all, the living and the dead, both the just and the unjust when the Son will judge us all, the living and the dead; the second coming of Christ that will bring new life. Matthews 16:27 states, "For the Son of man shall come in the glory of his Father with his angels; and then he shall reward every man according to his works" (NIV).

"I believe in Life Everlasting." In this final article, Article XII, I affirm my belief in Eternal life, which is the hope, a time when all of the injustices of this world will be wiped away.

According to Moltmann (2014), "The human being in his embodiment is not created to end in death; he is made for transformation through and beyond death. Hope for the resurrection of the body and a life everlasting in redemption corresponds to the bodily creation of the human being by God, and perfects that. The hope of resurrection is belief in a creation that gazes forward, to what is ahead (p. 275)." A view of Moltmann's eschatology, frees us as Pastoral Counselors, to be able to change the status quo. The energy (the push) for working for *justice* comes from the vision of working toward the promise, Eternal Life.

If we, all of humanity, had this energy and vision, injustice would be totally eradicated from this world. There would be no or less pain and suffering; fewer perpetrators and victims, less damage to our souls or the souls of others; freer to choose ways of being and relating that are rooted in love and lead to life and not death (Scazzero, 2010). Therefore, my role as an Angel of Soul Justice is to help those suffering understand the source of their pain and to work in collaboration with the client to find hope and love from a perspective of the love of the one, I call my God and creator of all of humanity; the *Creator and Author of Soul Justice*!!

My faith aligns with the Christian faith. This counselor has evidenced the powerful steadfast love of a God who delivers and provides comfort and healing through the good times and the bad times. As an Angel of Soul Justice, I am committed to guide my clients through stages of depression, anxiety and other sufferings. I must remember that God placed me in a position to be a Good Shepherd; *Soul Justifier* to my clients; to help them overcome their pain and suffering and arrive at a place of safety. Scazzero (2010) reminds, "The Lord tends to His flock like a shepherd: He gathers the lambs in his arms and carries them close to His heart; He gently leads those that have young." This counselor will be careful to follow the lead of the client and be flexible to understand the spirituality of all who may sit across from me in search of their own soul justice.

59

THEORETICAL APPROACH
CHAPTER 3

Critical Questions

During my continuous exploration of an appropriate integrative approach, questions centered on how I, as an Angel of Soul Justice could help individuals experience their own "Soul Justice". What approach or approaches could best identify with helping one to achieve a sense of wholeness? How could I help my client experience a true sense of worth that will enable them to redirect or channel negative energy into positive energy; to let go of self-pity and low self-esteem; to understand that they are justified in their search to recognize their significance in a world where equality or equity continues to appear out of reach. How could I help them regain their voice that was previously silenced through continuous physical, verbal and/or emotional abuse, move beyond the past and present and realize hope in the future? How could they become armored or empowered individuals, fully visible in their chosen or given society? What are the interventions that would allow one to perceive his or her pain and engage in a process to encourage one to move beyond the pain he/she experienced and declare freedom from being stuck in pain? These were critical questions that helped me to understand or decide on a preferred or best theoretical approach.

Integrative Psychotherapy

In answering the above questions, an integrative approach was the best theoretical approach to allow me to help individuals become armored or empowered individuals, fully visible in their chosen or given society regardless of their culture. Integrative psychotherapy covers a wide range of attitudes and perspectives as elements are drawn from different schools of psychotherapy in the treatment of a client. This approach is primarily concerned with theories instead of various techniques like the eclectic approach, which was an approach I had previously considered. The integrative therapist seeks to combine different theories into a new theory that is more comprehensive than any of the individual theories it has brought together. Integrative psychotherapy refers to the psychotherapeutic process of integrating the personality: uniting the "affective, cognitive, behavioral, and physiological systems within a person" (International Integrative Psychotherapy Association, 2016).

As an integrative psychotherapist, my way of understanding, way of being, and way of intervening is shaped from an integrative approach, which helps me to explore the "why and how" of the change as well. This approach helps me to lift up a diverse clientele such as those experiencing brokenness in our universe from all aspects of spirituality, cultural and socio-economic status. Every client's soul justice will not look, feel or smell the same. Spirituality will be an important component of the integrative approach. I agree with Carol Del Rio and Lyn White (2012) who argued that spirituality belongs to each person by virtue of being human. This spiritual constitution enables individuals to create or develop communities of faith. Hence, spirituality is not only sufficient but also necessary to discover what is transcendent. (pp. 123-142)

Cultural Perspective

Individuals from other faith traditions or cultures could find that an integrative approach could be a tool for change as it extends boundaries to encompass multitudes of beliefs and disciplines to create change and promote healthy living. This will extend the horizon to enable one to be an Angel of Soul Justice for a diverse and multicultural society; to help individuals redirect or channel negative energy into positive energy; to let go of self-pity and low self-esteem; to understand that one is justified in their search to recognize their significance in a world where equality is measured by those at the highest socio-economic level. During my years of internship, I had the opportunity to experiment in a healthful manner, a lot of research on multiple approaches to help me to understand how to be an effective agent of change for all of my clients. Those clients differed in many ways such as age, ethnicity/race, gender, geographical location or community, language, sexual orientation, spiritual/religious beliefs, socioeconomic situation, physical ability, and experience with traumatic situations. Each individual came in search of soul justice from an understanding based on their culture.

Culturally, I have found it important to gain insight regarding the best approach regardless of culture to help an individual experience a sense of trust and relaxation in the counseling environment.

This leads to the discussion of gaining or earning the trust of my clients; establishing a therapeutic alliance.

Establishing Therapeutic Alliance

As an Angel of Soul Justice, I seek to enter a relationship with my clients from a perspective of trust (nonjudgmental). Thus, my way of being must reflect nonjudgmental, empathetic understanding, congruence and unconditional positive regard for my client, to help ensure their self-concept become more positive and realistic. Carl Rogers described empathic orientation way of being, as an authentic, collaborative relationship, and being oneself in relation to another person (Broman, 2012). The client is the active narrator of meanings, goals, intentions, as it is their search of this meaning; for their soul justice, not my soul justice.

I have had the pleasure of working individually or in groups with African American males and females, Asian and Hispanic males, and White males. The importance of showing empathy, trust, and positive regard has been reinforced as a way of being while working with each of these groups. Trust issues are critical in working with African Americans and Africans, especially in the counseling arena. African Americans with Christianity as their faith foundation feel that seeking help from sources other than their Lord and Savior means they are questioning their faith regardless of their socio-economic status, especially individuals considered senior citizens. A recently published study by the American Psychological Association (2012) revealed that even young adult blacks with higher levels of education are significantly less likely to seek mental health services than whites of the same stature, citing stigma, lack of knowledge, trust and cultural understanding as key barriers (pp. 38-48),.

During my second year of internship, I worked with a middle age, middle income, African American female client, who had been court ordered to attend an Abuse Intervention Program. Establishing a therapeutic alliance that centered on trust, empathy and nonjudgmental was critical to helping her move beyond the pain he/she experienced and declares freedom from being stuck in pain; to experience soul justice. This individual had completed 14 weeks of a 20 weeks program that included several weeks of psychoeducational sessions of the Female Abuse Intervention Program. The presenting problem that brought her to this program was irrational behavior that caused both her and her ex-partner to receive injuries, and her to spend several days in jail. As a result of this irrational behavior, Client A, who had served several years in the U.S. Armed Forces and was gainfully employed, lost her job. She reported being embarrassed and experiencing a high degree of anxiety. Close to the end of our first session she tearfully unloaded a lot of details about her history. At the start of the fourth session, she thanked me for accepting her as a client for individual counseling. She stated that she felt better about herself. I asked her to share more. She stated that I was the reason that she felt better, reporting that she had been advised by others of many of the interventions we discussed, but she remained stuck and in pain. I again asked her to share more. She shared; it was something about my calming voice and nonjudgmental mannerism; my way of being, that helped her regain her sense of self-worth; that helped her experience a sense of trust and relaxation in the counseling environment. She shared that she heard the sincerity in my voice when I explained to her that her temporary irrational action did not diminish who she was as an individual nor discount her life accomplishments. Client A reported that she now felt ready to move forward with her head up and expected to be a source of support for others. She was ready to move beyond the pain and shame she had experienced and declare freedom from being stuck in life because of those two emotions. Client A had regained self-acceptance and her voice.

Way of Understanding

My way of understanding is shaped from my belief that for humanity to experience soul justice; redirect or channel negative energy into positive energy, we must focus on the things that we can control to help us to flourish in a fallen world. Therapeutic approaches that seem to be a strong fit to my way of understanding individuals include theories such as Adlerian and Cognitive Behavioral Therapeutic approaches. As a therapist, the secret to healing is to employ a therapeutic approach with an emphasis on human responsibility. A therapist must see individuals as teleological beings (with apparent purpose, or goal) and understand that the most central needs of persons are for belonging and purpose and worth *(soul justice);* these compare to the relational and dominion motives found in the creation story. The attainment of Soul Justice prepares one to go beyond the one-on-one counseling room to change society for the better, and this is a plus from a Christian perspective (Jones & Butman, 1991).

Thus, my goal is to gain understanding from an integrative approach that includes spirituality or just human faith as described by Paul Tillich (1957) in his book, Dynamics of Faith. In delineating his own definition of faith, Tillich (1957) defines faith as "the state of being ultimately concerned" and the dynamics of which are "the dynamics of man's ultimate concern" (p. 1).

Adlerian

Adlerian therapy places social interest as the highest intrinsic value. Charity which parallels social interest is among the premier Christian values, and no Christian can think of social interest without reflecting on "loving our neighbor as ourselves". But first of all, we must love ourselves. There cannot be a sense of crippling inferiority and brokenness; a sense of injustice. There can be no discrimination regarding our neighbor's culture, spirituality or lack of spirituality. What is critical is that we use our learned knowledge and experience to help others achieve positive goals so that they too can give back to society; so that they too can help someone experience soul justice. According to Jones and Butman (1991), Adlerian therapy suggests that cognitive change must yield practical fruit; "to be made new in the attitude of your minds and to put on the new self-created to be like God in true righteousness and holiness" Ephesians 4:24 (NIV).

Cognitive-Behavioral Theories

Cognitive-behavioral therapies are applicable in many diverse counseling settings including, church and family crisis, in which I conducted my two internships. Theorists like Ellis and Beck maintain that our thoughts influence our emotions and behaviors, so that the way we think determines how we feel and how we act. Soul Justice for me in middle school was reassigning my thought process from "I am inferior" to "I am equal and / superior". How I felt and responded to life and all of its challenges changed from negative to positive; at least positive in my thinking as to how to continue to flourish in a fallen world. Albert Ellis' ABC theoretical concept helps me work with a client's irrational belief using the simple phrase: "It depends on how you look at things" or "You can picture the glass as either half empty or half full." It then becomes their choice as to the linking of their feelings and thoughts. Will their choice help them to let go of self-pity and low self-esteem, or will their choice keep them shackled and bound in chains?

During my first year of internship, I experimented with Cognitive Behavioral Therapy (CBT) as a way of intervention. This meant that I had to learn to recognize the problem, belief system, origin of that belief system, mechanisms, and precipitant of presenting problem. My internship was at a restoration center of a church. The client came to counseling experiencing exhaustion, depression, and anger. The precipitant, financial distress, e.g., home in foreclosure, husband's inability to provide financial support, and having to rely on her elderly mother's retirement for a second source of income to qualify for the foreclosure prevention program led to the problem of underlying anger and disappointment with Jane's husband for lack of leadership and responsiveness. A second precipitant was her mother's threat to withdraw her name from the application process, stating the client needed to step up and be the woman of the house; to make sure the house was well managed and free of clutter.

The client's childhood experience led to her belief that parents had distinct roles; the father provided the financial support for the family, while the mother's role was to effectively manage the home and to safeguard the feelings of her husband even if it meant disregarding her true feelings. As a result of this belief, for several years, she engaged in patterns of behavior of cleaning up the home, maintaining finances, cooking, and sole breadwinner, which enabled her family members to avoid their responsibilities. This added to her sense of responsibility, exhaustion, and anger. Avoidance behavior that included withholding negative feelings from husband, sons and male boss led to problems of increased anger, depressive symptoms and marital problems.

After trying for several weeks to make strides with getting Jane to understand that spiritually, her coming to counseling was not a sign of a lost faith, I recommended the reading of Geri Scazzero's (2010), I Quit! Stop Pretending Everything is Fine and Change Your Life. Scazzero offered eight areas one might need to quit in order to pursue a healthy sense of balance emotionally, spiritually, psychologically, and vocationally: Quit Being Afraid of What Others Think, Quit Lying, Quit Dying to the Wrong Things, Quit Denying Anger, Sadness, and Fear, Quit Blaming, Quit Over-functioning, Quit Faulty Thinking, and Quit Living Someone Else's Life. In these areas, she used personal and biblical examples to show how "quitting" in these areas offered her soul justice and release and freedom from the overbearing and unhealthy demands on her life as a wife, mother, pastor, and leader. She did not shy away from her conviction that personal boundaries are healthy, necessary, and too often neglected for fear of not being seen as a "good Christian." I was hopeful that through a collaborative approach, this book would help the client draw on spiritual and other beliefs to allow her to think things through in a positive manner. It helped. I was relieved and grateful for an additional resource to help my client experience soul justice through self-care and other strategies that would enable her to be truthful to her husband regarding her anger. This external intervention tool helped the client to engage in a process that helped her identify themes that were applicable to her life and provided feedback from a spiritual perspective on the author's handling of each situation. The goal for the client was to resist "doing more than she should" and to find ways to incorporate her family into the process of accomplishing what was needed to achieve healthy boundaries for the client and her entire family.

A combination of establishing a strong alliance and applying cognitive behavioral techniques integrated with bibliotherapy and spirituality helped this client to understand the source of her reluctance to be truthful with her husband and the other members of her family and to become engaged in self-care with a renewed sense of self-worth.

Way of Intervening

Narrative Therapy Approach

There are times I find myself searching for a source of internal strength that a client can use to reach within to help gain understanding and or to alter the client's situation. This means that there is always a desire to learn as much as possible about my clients' lived experiences.

"Now is the time...to discover people's back stories. Learn to discover people's backgrounds. Ask and listen for the clues. Their histories reveal many things. They can explain fears and prejudices. They can unravel mysteries. They can give you warnings; or insights." (Lindsay, 2009, p. 170)

Narrative Therapy helps me to better understand my clients (victims and perpetrators), as this approach sees people as experts in their own lives and views problems as separate from people. I used this approach as intervention to help Client A understand that her irrational behavior did not identify her. According to White and Epston (1990), the principal premise of Narrative Therapy is that people develop mental health concerns when their personal narratives (their life journeys as seen and told from their personal perspectives) do not reflect their lived experiences. In other words, there is incongruity between "what should be happening" and "what is happening."

Reconstructing Self-Perspective

Client B revealed a narrative that described his mother as an arrogant drug addict and vain individual from whom he only derived his DNA. As a young child, his grandmother became his guardian angel and stepped in and removed him from his mother's home to make sure that he did not grow up in an environment where negative remarks, humiliation and inhuman criticism could rob him of self-esteem. He flourished in the positive environment of his grandmother's home, but would at times be exposed to the negative environment of his mother. Due to unexpected events, Client B's narrative placed him on an unwanted journey, traveling with a partner with characteristics similar to his description of his mother. These characteristics included drug addiction, arrogance and vanity (using others to get what she wanted). He stated that initially he felt that he could save or help his partner chart a different course of life, similar to what was done by a former family member, basically a narrative of giving back, but it instead led to moments of violence. The goal was to get Client B to look at ways of seeing himself in a different role; a role of strength and self-preservation. Identifying and deconstructing the problem narrative, externalizing the problem, mapping the effects of the problem and re-authoring B's story became the goal (Williams-Reade, Freitas, & Lawson, 2014). As Client B consistently spoke of his spirituality and Jesus Christ as his role model, the narrative technique known as life review, presented by LeFavi and Wessels (2003) as a spiritually-oriented life review process with overall goals of enhancing a client's psychological well-being and a sense of fulfillment became a likely intervention. This technique was used to help alter Client B's interpretation of a man's strength, which was tied to his concept of defending one's property and space with whatever means possible; usually physical and or verbal confrontation. This life review approach helped the client construct a preferred alternative story; handling conflict the way Jesus would handle it; effective communication.

In summary, an integrative approach of Adlerian, Cognitive Behavioral and Narrative Therapy along with spirituality helps me to be available to a diverse clientele seeking soul justice. This all begins with the establishment of a therapeutic alliance through a display of unconditional positive regard, congruence, and an empathic way of being, regardless of one's therapeutic approach to help individuals open up and be an effective and active agent in their search for meaning for their soul justice.

72

CRITIQUE AND FUTURE PLANS
CHAPTER 4

There is a saying 'Always welcome a stranger, you may be meeting an angel in disguise.' Hebrew 13:2 NIV "Do not forget to show hospitality to strangers, for by so doing some people have shown hospitality to angels without knowing it." This is a truism. Throughout the ages, in every religious or spiritual belief system, angels have walked amidst mankind to help, advise, protect and lead us to the Light. They may be unseen messengers, inhabiting the spirit world. Many are in the world in a physical body, dressed as befits the culture and country they inhabit. A guardian angel watches over our physical welfare. Angels help, inspire, and advise us through our higher self. Unfortunately, many individuals are unable to 'tune in' for this help, or simply ignore it. To attune to one's guardian angel can be literally a life-saving or life-altering experience. Mistakes are often avoided; we meet people not by chance but by design. Often there is work to do for mankind. These meetings are already planned prior to re-birth. (Archangels and Angels, 2016)

My years of experience in helping others on their journey toward healing have offered me a diversity of experiences. One year of internship experience was in a church environment, and the other year of experience occurred at a domestic violence family crisis center. At one location, all of the individuals voluntarily came because they or someone in the family recognized conflicts existed in their life. At the other location individuals primarily came because they were court ordered to attend an abuse intervention program, a victim program, or an anger management program. At the start of my first internship, I was afraid to encounter the journey. My fear was that I would do or say something that would be damaging to my clients' psyches. In spite of that fear, I pressed forward through sometimes bumpy flights. During those bumpy flights, I would look to my angels; my supervisors, my professors and classmates. They helped me navigate the turbulence and come to smooth landings. Riding through those bumpy flights enabled me to journey with my clients to softer landings on leveled wings.

Growing Edges

It was interesting and comforting to experience the growth that occurred over my two years of internship. The experience of my first case remains etched in my mind. My first client presented with nervous laughter. When I played back the tape and completed my verbatim, I noticed that I got caught up in the laughter. Other growing edges included lengthy paraphrasing and summarizations. I asked my peers and supervisor for suggestions as to how the laughter presented. The feedback was raw. In addition to the above-mentioned growing edges, the raw feedback uncovered the use of "go to" terminology "I hear you saying" followed by a "but" and "how does that make you feel?" Advice from peers and clinical supervisor included remaining calm and professional throughout the session to keep from getting sucked into the laughter, a congruent smile would be appropriate, and to utilize power words to keep my summary and other feedback simple (keep it simple). Other growing edges included the appropriateness of self-disclosure, the interruption of clients' sharing, and utilizing nuggets shared by the client. Let's just say, this Angel of Soul Justice's wings were totally clipped off. I was grounded and rightfully so!

During a Blue Christmas workshop later that semester, I became more conscious of my go to phrase "I hear you saying" followed by a "but". I was startled when I heard myself saying "but", at an inappropriate moment. I immediately reframed my phrase. Other feedback that I practiced during the Blue Christmas event was the appropriate times for laughter, smiles, interruptions and self-disclosure, and shortening my summarizations. I worked on listening for times when self-disclosure was appropriate while making sure there was a door to deflect back to the client's well-being. While it was critical for these individuals to hear a message from God, it was critical for these individuals to be heard, just as it is for all of my clients.

One of my clients during my first year of internship was a licensed counselor. While reading the intake summary, I began to immediately experience some anxieties regarding my ability to sit before this client. A review of the tape revealed my anxieties. Again, my peers were prepared to assist me in my struggle; to strengthen or clip my wings; whichever was appropriate according to what was witnessed. They shared a wide range of knowledge and observations that reinforced my wings to prepare me to help individuals experiencing pain and discomfort journey from an uncomfortable dimension to an environment where healing of the soul was the menu of the day. The growing edges from this case included: take a while to qualify my questions and to keep it simple, identify where the anxiety is playing out in the body, ask the client what worked for her in the past, when she felt anxious or needed to relax, keep the focus on client instead of other individuals discussed, concentrate on the heart, explore other demographic details such as age differences, the client stated she loved her work; explore what it is about her work she loved, and to be aware of all nonverbal symptoms. To minimize my anxiety, it was suggested that I place myself in the shoes of the counselor, trust my skills and review other tapes for my assurance. As stated earlier, this taping provided a learning opportunity for the entire class. The professor shared a large volume of information on how to handle anxiety and communication techniques that included: guided imagery, yawning, relaxation exercises, and Imago therapy. This information enabled me to sit with less anxiety with a seasoned professional counselor; to recognize that the client agreed to sit with me, even though she was aware that I was an intern. Also, she scheduled a follow up appointment stating she was committed to seeing me until her anxiety was minimized to a manageable level. Wing growth!

The client for my final case presentation of my first-year internship was also knowledgeable of the counseling profession even though they were not yet licensed. I utilized a cognitive behavioral approach to explore automatic thoughts, help reframe thought, and explore the origin of intermediate and core beliefs as it relates to group identity and the importance of self-care for all clients, including helping professionals. I asked the client about her strengths, utilized emotions, reminded her that "understanding behavior does not excuse it," simplified questions, and shortened my summarizations/ refection of meaning. Growth was realized.

My second year of internship at the family crisis center, involved working with individuals who were court ordered to attend group and individual abuse intervention and anger management programs that combined psychoeducational and counseling skills to combat domestic violence abuse. Most of the issues centered on anger management. It was time to apply the knowledge and skillset learned from my first year of internship to help smooth growing edges.

Growing edges during my second year of internship centered on improving my strategy of utilizing an integrated approach that included spirituality. The abuse intervention program at the crisis center required the application of the Duluth Model. The Duluth Model originated in 1981 from the Duluth Domestic Abuse Intervention Project in Duluth, Minnesota. This intervention proposed that the principal cause of domestic violence is a social and cultural patriarchal ideology that historically has allowed men to control women through power and violence. Violence perpetrated on women and children originates from their relative positions of weakness and vulnerability socially, politically, economically, and culturally. As such, the model does not assume that domestic violence is caused by mental or behavioral health problems, substance use, anger, stress, or dysfunctional relationships. The program concentrates on providing group facilitated exercises that challenge a male's perception of entitlement to control and dominate his partner. The Duluth Model is considered less of a therapy and more of a psychoeducational program for domestic violence perpetrators.

For my first individual case at the crisis center, in addition to the Duluth Model, I applied a cognitive behavioral approach with the integration of spirituality. I was uncomfortable trying to integrate a narrative therapy approach. Feedback from one peer during my case presentation was extremely valuable in helping me to begin the inclusion of narrative therapy. He shared the following:

> *"Your treatment plan contains some well-thought-out goals, objectives, and interventions to address your client's anger issues—especially the CBT oriented interventions. I would like to pose another view on the use of narrative therapy for this case. What if the client's problem narrative is that he is less valuable than others, and is, to a degree, unlovable? He could have formed these views from his family of origin due to having a verbally abusive and hateful mother, and an emotionally detached father and grandfather. He is in the midst of establishing a preferred narrative of being worthy, valuable and generative by serving others through his occupation, attempting to model himself after Jesus, and looking after the welfare of his son. It would be valuable to point out his progress along this new life path while identifying areas where he is struggling (which would likely be with self-esteem, self-love, and self-soothing."*
> *(Fabio* (Lomelino, 2016)

The above feedback gave me the confidence to go back to my initial plan to integrate narrative therapy as part of my treatment plan to help these individuals share their stories more fully and then explore ways to experience a different or preferred narrative for their future. It also made it easier to incorporate spirituality.

Finally, my growing edges included incorporating adequate time/attention to self-care (soul-care) in order to maintain healthy boundaries in the clinical relationship. I speak to this later in the section below on soul care.

Strengths

Supervisors, peers, and clients have shared that I am gifted with a calming presence. My personal and spiritual maturity have served as a positive factor in my being comfortable and able to quickly establish rapport with clients regardless of the client's culture or presenting problem. Throughout clinical supervision, I readily acknowledged and sought feedback on all aspects of my clinical work from my supervisors and peers. This facilitated growth. The growth gained during my first year internship allowed me to start my second year of internship with less stress and anxiety. It helped me to be comfortable and to meet my clients where they were.

One client, who was a repeat domestic abuse offender, expressed his strong belief in Jesus Christ. This individual afforded me an opportunity to learn more about my ability to be calm, and yet curious with my clients regardless of their situation. This Angel of Soul Justice understood that her role was to not be judgmental but to help this client work through a very complicated and dramatic series of events. This growth helped me to work with this client at his level of understanding and awareness to carefully integrate spirituality into his treatment plan as an extension of his narrative for understanding the past and how to navigate the future. The goal for each of these clients, perpetrators and victims was to provide a safe and compassionate space where they could speak about and process their difficult experiences.

Working with this population helped me to understand more about my gifts and role as an Angel of Soul Justice. I began to embrace and understand that my role as a Pastoral Counselor included working with the marginalized regardless of their story or situation. God placed me on this journey and had thus gifted me the ability to empathically connect with clients who had a history of domestic violence. This gift includes the wisdom, discernment, and skills to establish strong alliances that allowed me to use carefrontation with this population; to bring up personal insights, and to not back away if the client failed on the first or second attempt to acknowledge them, but to keep pressing until points sank home. My approach involved challenging one's thoughts and behaviors to increase their awareness and insight. My work with clients who had a reported history of verbal and physical aggression required care and empathy and not signs of intimidation. God kept me surrounded by His angels who also surrounded each of my clients.

Because of God's affirmation, I never experienced fear or intimidation, but instead peace while working with victims of domestic abuse and providing them a safe space to share their untold stories. I had a client who had experienced a wide range of inflicted trauma that included multiple generational rapes, pain, and conflict that spoke to the themes of guilt, shame and mistrust that had been kept secret for so many years. This story crystallized the reason I aspired to become a Pastoral Counselor; to journey with others through the darkness and suffering to help them emerge within the light; finding a voice to share their story and pain. The courage to not walk away from these events was realized. This same courage and bravery are required to work for all populations, not just this population. To be able to empathize I must expose myself to the pain, misery, or horror they experience.

Throughout my two years of internship and experiences as a licensed graduate professional counselor (LGPC), I learned to be open to critical feedback from others and to not receive the feedback as personal criticism. This strength helped me to realize growth from my first case presentation, clients as a LGPC and LCPC. My knowledge base expanded tremendously from a therapeutic perspective along with the integration of spirituality, not just from feedback but from articles that professors have provided as a result of each case presented and clarifications requested by our class. This includes a better understanding and experience for using the DSM-5 to determine the correct diagnosis to help guide treatment for my clients (to become a more effective change agent).

Soul Care

As stated, several times above, one of my growing edges is self-care (my own soul care). As a counselor and manager who has a full-time job of 40 plus hours a week, mother, grandmother, wife and church leader active in ministry; the bar of achieving self-care continues to move beyond my reach. Self-care belongs to the body, soul, spirit, and mind.

I agree with Maynard and Parker (2015, p. 48) who stated, "Pastoral counselors are poised to serve as bridge builders and integrators between the historical practices of pastoral counseling and the increasingly professionalized and guild-based world of mental health." While I am happy to be a part of this bridge building, at the same time, I must keep in mind that self-care (my soul care) is real and it is critical to survival. Humanity has limitations where God is infinite. This means rest and honoring the Sabbath. This may require quitting or letting go of some projects; those projects that may cause me to lose balance. The kind of quitting I'm talking about isn't about weakness or giving up in despair. It is about the strength to live in the truth (integrity). It is about understanding what my assignment is. Again, Geri Scazzero (2010) states it best:

> *"Biblical quitting goes hand in hand with choosing. When we quit those things that are damaging to our souls or the souls of others, we are freed up to choose other ways of being and relating that are rooted in love and lead to life. When we quit for the right reasons, we are changed...The Holy Spirit births a new resolve within us" (self-efficacy).* (Scazzero, 2010, p. 16)

Ecclesiastes 3:1 says *"There is a season for everything under the heaven."* Quitting is a season. While this Angel of Soul Justice will never quit, she must call to memory Gospel songs and phrases that include: *"Stand still and know that I am God"* and *"This Battle is Not Mine, It's the Lord"* I must stand still to recognize whether an assignment is mine, a referral or requires consultation.

Since becoming a seminarian student in January 2005 followed by a Pastoral Counselor student in January 2012, I longed to enjoy a Sabbath, even after completing both Master's degrees. Practicing Sabbath would fulfill my desire to set apart one day for simple rest and quiet worship of God. Adele Calhoun (2005) defines Sabbath as "God's gift of repetitive and regular rest that is given for our delight and communion with God" (p. 13). I am a living example of Haley Barton's (2006) statement "If we do not allow for a rhythm of rest in our overly busy lives, illness becomes our Sabbath – our pneumonia, our cancer, our heart attack, our accidents create Sabbath for us." (p. 131). I am mandated by God to take a Sabbath, "Remember the Sabbath day by keeping it holy. Six days you shall labor and do all your work, but the seventh day is a Sabbath to the Lord your God" (Exodus 20: 8-10, NIV). Practicing the discipline of Sabbath would grant me freedom from the addiction to busyness, rush and hurry; make me acknowledge my human limits and live within them; honor the way God created me by living a healthy and intentionally rested life; live a weekly rhythm of rest followed by six days of work; delight in God, family, the seasons, meals and all good gifts of creation; and trust God for all that I am not doing and taking care of on Sunday (Haley-Barton, 2006, pp. 131-145). I long deeply to sit alone and read a book just to enjoy it; not because I am required to write a paper, prepare for a discussion, presentation, or an exam.

To manage my feelings, as a counselor and leader I must be aware of my emotions (depression, anger, hostility, grief and loss, fear, and bitterness) and understand their origin, self-awareness. I must develop strategies to manage these emotions. Self-awareness in important for me to learn to calibrate my self-expectations. Self-understanding informs me of my talent potential, my personality strengths, and physical abilities. Self-management will help me as a spiritual leader and pastoral counselor to be in touch with followers and clients' expectations of me. When I am healthy, I will be able to shape expectations about my performance and leadership rather than meet them. One's success grows out of one's ability to have a "well managed life" (McNeal, pp. 35-60). My success as an Angel of Soul Justice will depend on my ability to be a resilient clinician.

Enhancing Resiliency

"Therapists must establish mechanisms to maintain their own physical and mental health and ways to get relief from the intensity of the work...one such mechanism is to have professional outlets, such as supervision and consultation, to provide information, perspective, and support. Another is to have personal outlets for sustenance and recreation away from the work setting." (Courtois, 2002)

Robert Wicks, (2008) stated that "although being a clinician is a wonderful way to devote oneself to the welfare of others, unless care is taken to ensure that the rest of one's life is fulfilling and balanced as well, one's life becomes too narrow, limited, and eventually distorted" (p. 43). I look forward to intentionally applying many of the self-care protocols shared for renewing oneself on a daily basis. These include:

"Quiet walks by yourself, time and space for meditation, spiritual and recreational reading – including the diaries, some light exercise, opportunities to laugh offered by movies, cheerful friends, etc., a hobby such as playing tennis, phone calls to family and friends who inspire and tease you, involvement in projects that renew, and listening to music you enjoy." (Wicks, 2008, p. 47)

The Flight Forward

Moving forward included gaining additional supervisory knowledge as I focused on my 2000 hours necessary to become a licensed pastoral counselor, licensed Angel of Soul Justice to help others earn, repair or strengthen their wings to help them navigate their flight of purpose. Philippians 3: 12-16, NIV reads:

"Not that I have already obtained all this, or have already arrived at my goal, but I press on to take hold of that for which Christ Jesus took hold of me. Brothers and sisters, I do not consider myself yet to have taken hold of it. But one thing I do: Forgetting what is behind and straining toward what is ahead, I press on toward the goal to win the prize for which God has called me heavenward in Christ Jesus. All of us, then, who are mature should take such a view of things. And if on some point you think differently, that too God will make clear to you. Only let us live up to what we have already attained."

I graduated from Loyola University, Pastoral Counseling program, May 2016. August 2016, I was offered the opportunity to assist one of my previous internship supervisors expand her counseling business into Southern Maryland while still working full-time with the U. S. Census Bureau. August 23, 2018, I received my documents from the Maryland State Board of Professional Counselors and Therapists certifying me as a Licensed Clinical Professional Counselor (LCPC). July 1, 2021, I opened my own counseling practice, DBD Counseling Services. I am fully aware that my total commitment is to God and His purpose.

It appears that total commitment as an Angel of Soul Justice, means I must be flexible, even as I continue to broaden my cultural horizon, self-awareness, step into liminal spaces, and continue my career development in multiple areas that include seeking out others of various diverse demographics that include race, ethnicity, socio-economic status and other differences, going on mission trips, etc. This will provide me a small sense of understanding from a personal perspective, as I am aware that only being a visitor in another's environment other than my own is not the same as permanently journeying in that environment. This will allow me to practice Sawubona, meaning "I see you." More than words of politeness, Sawubona carries the importance of recognizing the worth and dignity of each person. It says, "I see the whole of you-your experiences, your passions, your pain, your strengths and weaknesses, and your future." (Sawubona! Loom International, 2022).

One's understanding of God's message of love and stewardship affects one's attitudes and regard for all of humanity and nature. I believe that interpretation or misinterpretation of theology across faith communities has contributed to the imbalance of equilibrium with respect to humanity to humanity and nature. My experiences attending other religious worship services have proved to be very enlightening. I have always felt safe and welcome regardless of the race, ethnicity, community, or faith of the chosen or nearest congregation. Just as God is the center of my worship experience, He appeared to be the center of each of the worship arenas I attended. We worshipped in angelic harmony. The same is required of me in the counseling arena.

87

Summary

In summary, Parsons, the father of career counseling laid the groundwork for consideration of the context of a person and the environment in his three-step process. These are: 1) develop a clear understanding of yourself, your attitudes, interests, ambitions, resource limitations, and other qualities; 2) develop a knowledge of the requirements and conditions of success, advantages and disadvantages, compensation, opportunities, and 3) prospects in different lines of work' use "true reasoning" on the relations of these two groups of facts (Amundson, Harris-Bowlsbey, & Niles, 2014). A career role is a vehicle through which to express and fulfill one's life work. Instead of being caught up in defending our position, we must concentrate on accomplishing the mission (our God given purpose) (Boldt, 2009).

My career roles have allowed me, Dora Durante, to express and fulfill my life's career in a wide range of activities, visiting my grandmother during the summer and working in the cotton and tobacco fields of Marion, South Carolina culminating at this point as a Licensed Clinical Professional Counselor and manager for the U.S Census Bureau advocating programs for sensitizing the collection of data for individuals experiencing homelessness and other special populations, along with walking into God's designed purpose as Pastoral Counselor, owner of DBD Counseling Services as of July 1, 2021.

I cannot say that each of my career choices was influenced by my spiritual or religious identity. Some of these careers just happened. I planned for my first career choice, chemical laboratory technician by earning a degree in chemistry. As stated above, my second career was the result of sickness forcing me out of my first career choice. My third career was happenstance. Even though I do not feel that my spiritual or religious identity influenced these choices, it is my belief that God as the Master chess mover was orchestrating my life, moving me (chess pieces) to this greater place of Zion to do His will; to help heal broken humanity.

It is my belief that God placed me on this journey to be a change agent in the venue of His choosing; a messenger of healing and restoration to the marginalized; to advocate on their behalf. This requires me to remain equipped to answer to God's assigned workload; an Angel of Soul Justice witnessing God's suffering creation being lifted up by the wings of "His Messenger" and filled with both positive energy and potential that motivates self-acceptance and self-care.

Biography

Dora Durante is a Licensed Clinical Professional Counselor (LCPC), with a concentration in Spirituality and Pastoral Counseling. She is board certified through the National Board of Certified Counselors, with a number of other certifications that include: Telehealth for Mental Health Professionals, and Prepare/ Enrich Facilitator. Dora is the founder of

DBD Counseling Services as of July 1, 2021. She started her own counseling business with the awareness that God placed her in a position to be a Good Shepherd; Soul Justifier to her clients; to help them overcome their pain and suffering and arrive at a place of safety.

Dora's training and experiences as an intern and licensed clinical professional counselor, a teacher, and her work with the Department of Commerce enable her to be available to a diverse clientele seeking soul justice in the form of healing, applying an integrative therapeutic approach. She defines soul justice as the proper and lawful healing of one's brokenness from the inside out, a healing process from pain and destruction that produces life (joy, peace, happiness, and self-worth). Her encounters as an intern and licensed counselor with adolescents, young, middle age, and elderly adults across multiple socio-economic ranges and ethnicities, Africans, African Americans, Asians, Europeans, and English-speaking Hispanics have enlarged her awareness that a diverse population encompasses a multitude of belief systems and norms, requiring active listening. Through this process of active listening, individuals will be able to experience their true nature, realize hope and find Soul Justice creatively, spiritually, and compassionately.

92

References

Achtenemeier, P. J., Boraas, R. S., Fishbane, M., Perkins, P., & Walker, Jr., W. O. (Eds.). (1996). *The harpercollins bible dictionary*. New York, NY: HarperSanFrancisco.

Amundson, N., Harris-Bowlsbey, J., & Niles, S. (2014). *Essential elements of career counseling: Processes and techniques* (3rd ed.). Upper Saddle River: Pearson.

Aquileana. (2014). *Plato: The republic: on the concept of justice.* Retrieved December 2015, from https://aquileana.wordpress.com/2014/03/29/plato-the-republic-on-the-concept-of-justice/

Archangels and Angels. (2016, April 17). Retrieved April 17, 2016, from www.ofspiritandsoul: http://www.ofspiritandsoul.com/angels.html

Boldt, L. G. (2009). *Zen and the art of making a living: A practical guide to creative career design* (2010 ed.). New York: Penguin Books.

Broman, C. L. (2012, February 22). Race differences in the receipt of mental health services among young adults. *Psychological Services, 9*(1), 38-48. doi:10.1037/a0027089

Calhoun, A. A. (2005). *Spiritual disciplines handbook: Practices that transforms us.* Downers Grove, Illinois: InterVarsity Press.

Calhoun, A. A. (2005). Spiritual Disciplines Handbook: Practices That Transforms Us. . In A. A. Calhoun, *Spiritual Disciplines Handbook: Practices That Transforms Us.* (p. 13). Downers Grove, Illinois: InterVarsity Press.

Carlson, J., & Rohn, C. R. (1989). *Christianity, patriarchy, and abuse.* Cleveland: The Pilgrim Press.

Coogan, M. D. (2001). *The new oxford annotated bible: new revised standard version with the apocrypha.* New York, NY: Oxford Universityy Press.

Costella, R. B. (Ed.). (1991). *Random house webster dictionary.* New York, NY: Random House.

Courtois, C. A. (2002). *Recollections of sexual abuse: Treatment principles and guidelines.* W. W. Norton, Incorporated.

DeBose, T. L. (2012, July 7). Black women in america: Their faith is their bedrock. *Washington Post*, A1, A6. Washington, District of Columbia, USA: Washington Post.

Haley-Barton, R. (2006). *Sacred rhythms: Arranging our lives for spiritual transformation.* Downers Grove, Illinois: InterVarsity Press.

Historic Church Documents. (2006, December 1). Retrieved from Center for reformed theology and apologetics: http://www.refomed.org/documents/apostles_creed. html

International Integrative Psychotherapy Association. (2016). Retrieved from International Integrative Psychotherapy Association: http://integrativeassociation.com/english/association

Johnson, J. W. (1927, renewed 1955, December 5). *God's trombones: Seven negro sermons in verse.* New York, NY: Viking Press, Inc. Retrieved from www.bartleby.com/269/December 5, 2015

Jones, S. L., & Butman, R. E. (1991). *Modern psycho-therapies: A comprehensive christian appraisal.* Downers Grove, IL: InterVarsity Press.

King, M. L. (1963). *Letter from a birmingham jail.* Retrieved December 2015, from http://www.uscrossier.org/pullias/wp-content/uploads/2012/06/king.pdf

Kozol, J. (2001). *Ordinary resurrections.* New York: Perennial.

LeFavi, R. G., & Wessels, M. H. (2003). Life review in pastoral counseling: Background and efficacy for use with the terminally ill. *The Journal of Pastoral Care and Counseling, 57*(3), 281-292.

Lindsay, P. (2009). *Now is the time:170 ways to seize the moment.* New York, NY: MFJ Books.

Lomelino, F. (2016, February 12). Feedback to case presentation. *Loyola Supervision Class PC 664.* Columbia, Maryland.

Martin Luther King, J. (1963, August 28). *I have a dream.* Retrieved April 17, 2016, from Puritan Hard Drive: http://www.americanrhetoric.com/speeches/mlkihaveadream.htm

Maynard, E. A., & Snodgrass, J. L. (Eds.). (2015). *Understanding pastoral counseling.* New York, New York: Springer Publishing Company.

McNeal, R. (2006). Practicing Greatness: 7 Disciplines of Extraordinary Spiritual Leaders. In R. McNeal, *Practicing Greatness: 7 Disciplines of Extraordinary Spiritual Leaders* (pp. 35-61). San Francisco, CA: Jossey-Bass Press.

McNeal, R. (n.d.). *Practicing greatness: 7 disciplines of extraordinary spiritual leaders.* San Francisco, CA: Jossey-Bass Press.

Moltmann, J. (2014). *Jurgen Moltmann: Collected Readings.* (M. Kohl, Ed.) Minneapolis, Minnesota: Fortress Press.

Pargament, K. I. (2011). *Spiritually integrated psychotherapy: Understanding and addressing the sacred.* New York, NY: The Guilford Press.

Rio, C. M., & White, L. J. (2012). Separating spirituality from religiosity: A hylomorphic attitudinal perspective. *Psychology of Religion and Spirituality, 4*(2), 123-142. doi:10.1037/a0027552

Sawubona! Loom International. (2022, December 09). Retrieved from Sawubona!: www.loominternational.org/sawubona/

Scazzero, G. (2010). *I Quit! Stop pretending everything is fine.* Grand Rapids, MI: Zondervan.

Shopshire, H., & Stroghlin (Eds.). (2008). *I was in prison: united methodist perspectives on prison ministry.* Nashville, TN: General Board Of Higher Education and Ministry.

Somebody Cares Malawi. (2014, December 2). Retrieved from http://www.somebodycaresmalawi.org/: http://www.somebodycaresmalawi.org/

Tillich, P. (1957). *Dynamics of faith* (Vol. 577). (P. Classics, Ed.) New York: New York: HarperCollins.

Tillich, P. (1957). *Dynamics of Faith* (Vol. 577). (P. Classics, Ed.) New York: New York: HarperCollins.

White, E. G. (2011). *Counsel to parents, teachers, and students.* Nampa, ID: Pacific Press Publishing Associations.

White, M., & Epson, D. (1990). *Narrative means to therapeutic ends.* New York: Norton.

Whitney, D. S. (1991). Spiritual Disciplines for the Christian Life. In D. S. Whitney, *Spiritual Disciplines for the Christian Life* (pp. 41-46). Colorado: NavPress.

Wicks, R. J. (2008). *The resilient clinician.* New York, NY: Oxford University Press.

Williams, D. S. (1993). *Sisters in the wilderness: The challenge of womanist God-talk.* New York: Orbis Book.

Williams-Reade, J., Freitas, C., & Lawson, L. (2014). Narrative-informed medical family therapy:Using narrative therapy practices in brief medical encounters. *Family, Systems, & Health, 32*(4), 416-425.